DIY SOLAR PROJECTS
for Beginners

Quarto.com

© 2025 Quarto Publishing Group USA Inc.
Text © 2011 Quarto Publishing Group USA Inc.

First Published in 2025 by New Shoe Press, an imprint of The Quarto Group,
100 Cummings Center, Suite 265-D, Beverly, MA 01915, USA.
T (978) 282-9590 F (978) 283-2742

Essential, In-Demand Topics, Four-Color Design, Affordable Price
New Shoe Press publishes affordable, beautifully designed books covering evergreen, in-demand subjects. With a goal to inform and inspire readers' everyday hobbies, from cooking and gardening to wellness and health to art and crafts, New Shoe titles offer the ultimate library of purposeful, how-to guidance aimed at meeting the unique needs of each reader. Reimagined and redesigned from Quarto's best-selling backlist, New Shoe books provide practical knowledge and opportunities for all DIY enthusiasts to enrich and enjoy their lives.

Visit Quarto.com/New-Shoe-Press for a complete listing of the New Shoe Press books.

New Shoe Press titles are also available at discount for retail, wholesale, promotional, and bulk purchase. For details, contact the Special Sales Manager by email at specialsales@quarto.com or by mail at The Quarto Group, Attn: Special Sales Manager, 100 Cummings Center, Suite 265-D, Beverly, MA 01915, USA.

10 9 8 7 6 5 4 3 2 1

ISBN: 978-0-7603-9812-8
eISBN: 978-0-7603-9813-5

The content in this book was previously published in *DIY Solar Projects* (2011 Cool Springs Press) by Eric Smith.

Library of Congress Cataloging-in-Publication Data available

Lead Photographer: Corean Kormarec
Set Builder: James Parmeter

Printed in China

NOTICE TO READERS

For safety, use caution, care, and good judgment when following the procedures described in this book. The publisher cannot assume responsibility for any damage to property or injury to persons as a result of misuse of the information provided. The techniques shown in this book are general techniques for various applications. In some instances, additional techniques not shown in this book may be required. Always follow manufacturer's instructions included with products, since deviating from the directions may void warranties. The projects in this book vary widely as to skill levels required: some may not be appropriate for all do-it-yourselfers, and some may require professional help. Consult your local building department for information on building permits, codes, and other laws as they apply to your project.

DIY SOLAR PROJECTS
for Beginners

Small and Easy Projects to Whole-Home Systems That Use the Sun

ERIC SMITH

NEW SHOE PRESS

Contents

Introduction

Every hour of every day enough solar energy falls on the Earth to supply the entire planet with power for a year. The energy is completely free and non-polluting; there's no danger of an oil spill, no mountaintop removal, no toxic waste, no smog, no nuclear meltdowns, and no monthly bill. Plus, it will keep coming for at least a few billion years.

The only catch is that we haven't entirely figured out how to harvest as much as we need. We're making progress, but we're not there yet.

This book is a primer on how you can begin. You don't have to stand on the sidelines waiting for scientists to invent the perfect solar cell. There are cost-effective, efficient ways to harvest solar energy right now. Solar cookers, solar hot water heaters and solar hot air collectors, to name a few, can all be made using standard building materials available from home centers, and they save money and energy right away. Even photovoltaic panels, which are still widely thought to be too expensive for the average homeowner, sometimes wind up being cheaper than conventional power after you factor in rebates, tax credits and money earned when you generate more electricity than you use. And if you live (or would like to live!) off the grid, solar cells are actually the cheapest power source.

The term "solar power" is really a bit misleading. Solar power is not just big arrays of solar panels. There are two essential strategies for harnessing solar power. The first uses photovoltaic cells to convert light to electricity; depending on the size and number of panels, cells can power anything from a pocket calculator to an entire city. However, the basic building block–the cells– have to be manufactured. The second type of solar power involves concentrating and converting sunlight to heat; the technology to do that is simple enough to be understood by children, relatively inexpensive, and very DIY friendly. If you can glue aluminum foil to cardboard or cover a wooden box with a piece of glass you can make a working solar collector and start saving real money immediately.

In this book we'll explore both types of solar power, explaining how-to projects that you can build with basic tools and skills. We'll show you how to heat your own water, warm up your house, dry your own lumber, make your own distilled water and do other projects that turn solar heat into reduced utility bills. We'll also explain the basics of solar electricity, from battery charging and simple lights and pumps to sophisticated whole-house systems, and show you simple ways you can make use of solar electric technology right now.

Most home centers carry all the materials you need to get started with solar thermal projects like hot water heaters, and some sell solar panels and plug-and-play systems. If you want to go further and jump into more complex projects, you can find suppliers in the Resource Guide who will help you put together anything from a battery-charging station to a large, whole-house solar system.

The sun is shining. Let's get started.

A Look into the Future

Solar technology is advancing rapidly, but the basic ideas behind it have been around for a very long time. More than two thousand years ago, Greeks, Romans, Chinese and others were starting fires by concentrating and focusing the rays of the sun, and structures have been built and oriented to collect—or block—solar heat for at least that long. The first known solar cooker was used in the 1830s, and the first solar cell was developed in 1876. The photo-electric effect—the process whereby light creates electricity—was explained by Albert Einstein in 1905. Turning the abundant sunlight that falls on the earth every day into useful energy is a dream that has been pursued for centuries, but only recently has manufacturing technology advanced to the point where these dreams can begin to be realized by almost anyone.

Fossil fuels are slowly but very definitely running out, even as the world's energy needs increase. All the fossil fuel that will ever be available on earth, including uranium for nuclear power, is less than half of the amount of solar energy received on earth every year. And solar energy will never run out.

All over the world scientists are experimenting with new materials and techniques to harvest this energy, and new ways to improve the efficiency of materials being used now, such as silicon. Photo-synthesis in plants is being studied for clues about how to make better solar cells, since plants make much more efficient use of the sun's energy than silicon cells currently do. Fuel cells, which can use solar power to convert water into hydrogen fuel using solar or other renewable power, are being researched as an alternative to batteries. Even impossible-sounding ideas like placing giant solar panel arrays in orbit, where they can harvest ten times as much power as they do on earth, are being seriously considered.

Even though we don't yet know what it will look like or what the infrastructure that makes it work on a large scale will look like, solar technology is our future.

OPPOSITE TOP LEFT: Solar panels are combined with solar hot water collectors (the panels along the ridge) to provide electricity, hot water and heat for this home.

OPPOSITE TOP RIGHT: Solar power plants are most cost-effective in parched desert areas where the sky is usually clear. This array provides power for an air force base in Nevada.

OPPOSITE BOTTOM: With a few photovoltaic panels and storage batteries, isolated areas miles off the electric grid, like this village on Surin Island in Thailand, can have reliable power for modern convenience.

Solar Electricity

When NASA scientists of the 1950s needed a revolutionary source of power for their spacecraft, they had to look and think beyond the earth. Their challenge was monumental, yet their solution poetically simple: They would find a way to tap into the most abundant, most accessible, and most reliable source of energy in the solar system—the sun.

Producing your own electricity with photovoltaics, or PV, is certainly one of the most exciting and rewarding ways of going green. Homeowners everywhere are using the sun to generate electrical power, and also to heat water for their showers, heating systems, and even swimming pools. The economic benefits can be significant, and when you consider that supplying the average home with conventional power creates over three tons of carbon emissions each year (over twice that of the average car), the environmental benefits of pollution-free solar energy are nothing to squint at.

This chapter introduces you to the most popular solar options for supplementing your existing systems or even declaring energy independence by taking your home "off the grid." As solar technology continues its journey from the space program to suburban rooftops and beyond, anyone serious about climbing aboard will find a vibrant new marketplace that's more than ready to help.

IN THIS CHAPTER

With every passing year, solar panels become more efficient and less expensive. The day when a solar panel array is installed on every roof to provide power for the home and for the larger electrical grid may not be too far off.

The Solar-Powered Home

Residential PV systems supply electricity directly to a home through solar panels mounted on the roof or elsewhere. These are essentially the same systems that pioneering homeowners installed back in the 1970s. In those days, however, panels were less efficient and much more expensive than the average of $9 per watt today (and people in many areas can cut that number in half with renewable-energy rebates and tax credits).

Here's how PV power works: A solar panel is made up of small solar cells, each containing a thin slice of silicon, the same material used widely in the computer industry. Silicon is an abundant natural resource extracted from the earth's crust. It has semi-conductive properties, so that when light strikes the positive side of the slice, electrons try to move to the negative side. Connecting the two sides with a wire creates an electrical circuit and a means for harnessing this electrical activity.

Solar cells are grouped together and connected by wires to create a module, or panel. Modules can be installed in a series to create a solar "array." The size of an array, as well as the quality of the semiconductor material, determines its power output.

The electricity produced by solar cells is DC, or direct current, which is what most batteries produce (and what battery-powered devices run on). Most household appliances and light fixtures run on AC, or alternating current, electricity. Therefore, PV systems include an inverter that converts the DC power from the panels to AC power for use in the home. It's all the same to your appliances, and they run just as well on solar-generated power as on standard utility power.

Solar electric panels provide all the power for this super-efficient house.

Grid-Connected & Off-the-Grid Systems

Home PV systems can be designed to connect to the local utility network (the power grid) or to supply the home with all of its electricity without grid support. There are advantages and disadvantages to each configuration.

In a grid-connected setup, the utility system serves as a backup to supply power when household demand exceeds the solar system's capacity or during the hours when the sun is down. This elimates the need for batteries or a generator for backup, and makes grid-connected systems simpler and less expensive than off-the-grid systems. One of the best advantages of grid connection is that when the solar system's output exceeds the house's demand, excess power is delivered back to the grid and the homeowner often gets credit for every watt produced. This is called net-metering and is guaranteed by law in many states; however, not every state requires utility companies to offer it, and not all companies offer the same payback. Some simply let the meter roll backwards, essentially giving you full retail value for the power, while others buy back power at the utility's standard production price—much less than what they charge consumers.

The main drawbacks of being tied to the grid are that you may still have to pay service charges for the utility connection even if your net consumption is zero, and you're still vulnerable to power outages at times when you're drawing from the grid. But the convenience of grid backup along with the lower cost and reduced maintenance of grid-connected systems make them the most popular choice among homeowners in developed areas.

Off-the-grid, or standalone, systems serve as the sole supply of electricity for a home. They include a large enough panel array to meet the average daily demand of the household. During the day, excess power is stored in a bank of batteries for use when the sun is down or when extended cloud cover results in low output. Most standalone systems also have a gas-powered generator as a separate, emergency backup.

For anyone building a new home in an undeveloped area, installing a complete solar system to provide your own power can be less expensive than having the utility company run a line out to the house (beyond a quarter-mile or so, new lines can be very costly). There are some maintenance costs such as battery replacement, but it's possible to save a lot of money in the long run, and never having to pay a single electric bill is deeply satisfying to off-the-grid homeowners.

As mentioned, off-the-grid systems are a little more complicated than grid-connected setups. There are the batteries to care for, and power levels have to be monitored to prevent excessive battery run-down and to know when generator backup is required. To minimize power demands, off-the-grid homes tend to be highly energy-efficient. Installing super-efficient appliances is a major step towards making a smaller, less expensive solar array satisfy the home's energy needs. Smaller steps, such as connecting chargers and other electronic devices

Polycrystalline silicon is used in almost all photovoltaic panels to convert photons of light into electricity.

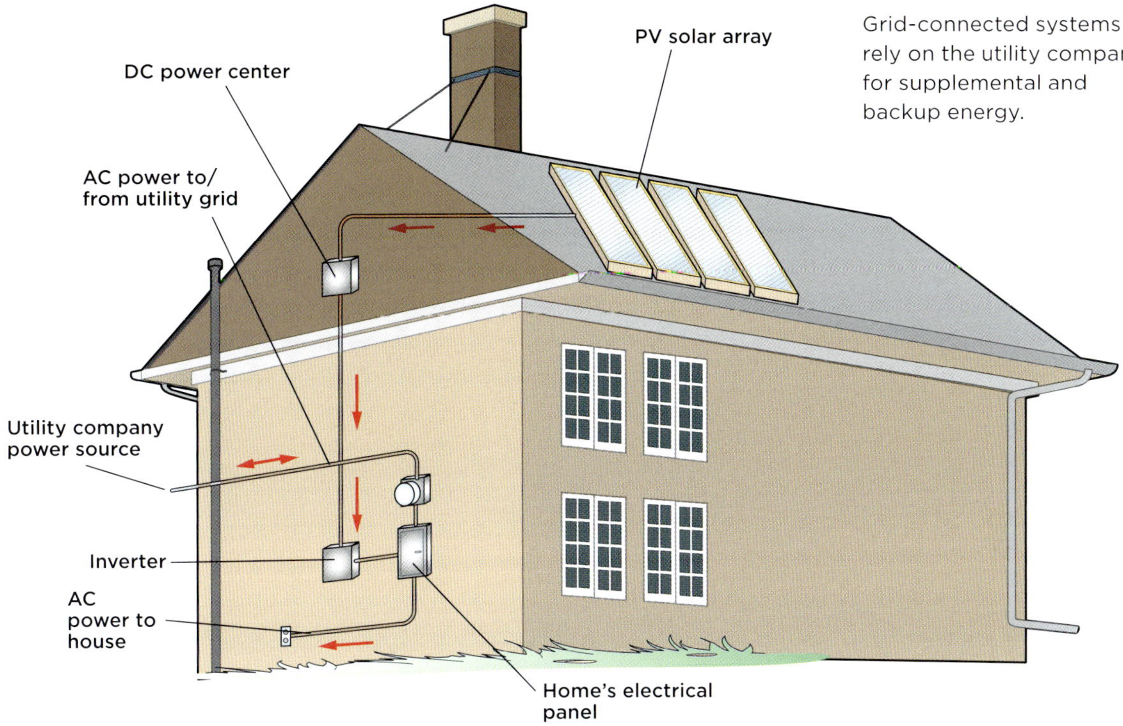

DC power center

AC power to/ from utility grid

PV solar array

Grid-connected systems rely on the utility company for supplemental and backup energy.

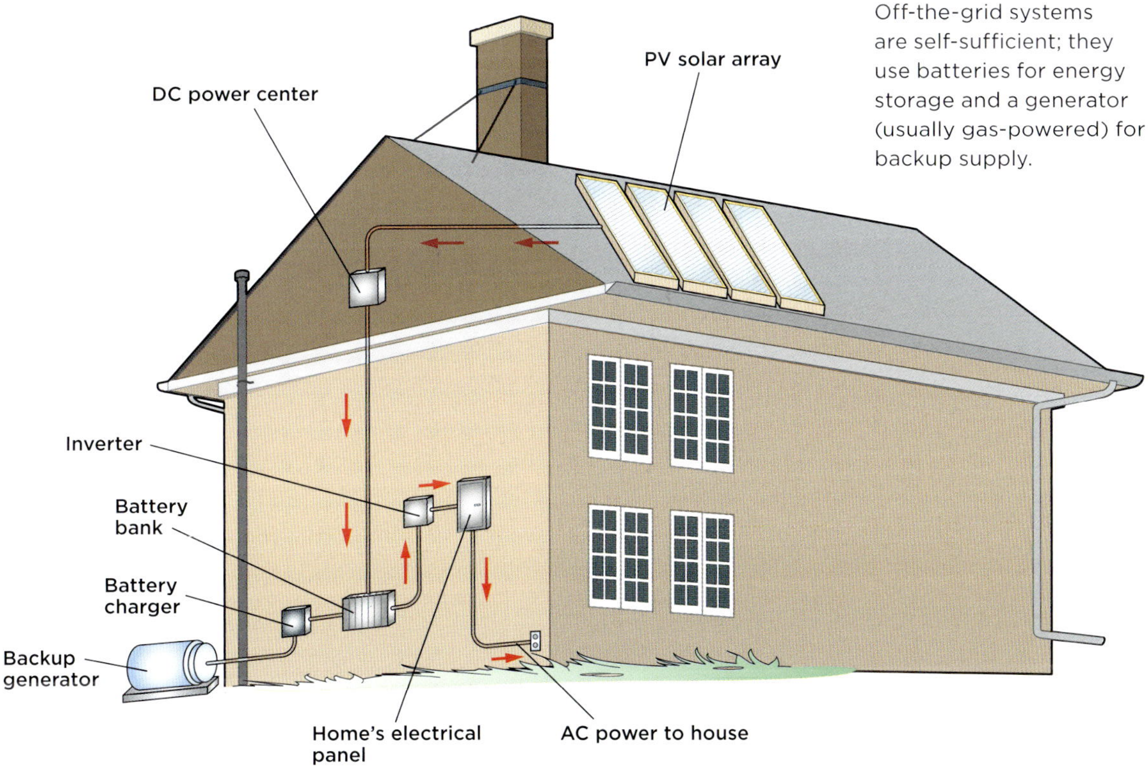

Utility company power source

Inverter

AC power to house

Home's electrical panel

DC power center

PV solar array

Off-the-grid systems are self-sufficient; they use batteries for energy storage and a generator (usually gas-powered) for backup supply.

Inverter

Battery bank

Battery charger

Backup generator

Home's electrical panel

AC power to house

Mounting solar arrays on the ground offers greater flexibility in placement when rooftop installation is impractical, or is prohibited by local building codes or homeowners associations.

to a power strip that can be turned off when the devices are not in use, also help by eliminating small but cumulative energy losses. If you're interested in taking your home off the grid, talk with as many experts and off-the-grid homeowners as you can. Their experiences can teach you invaluable lessons for successful energy independence.

Solar Panel Products

PV modules come in a range of types for different applications and power needs. The workhorse of the group is the glass- or plastic-covered rigid panel that can be mounted to the roof of a house or other structure, on an exterior wall, or on the ground at various distances from the house. Panel arrays can also be mounted onto solar-powered tracking systems that follow the sun for increased productivity.

Rigid modules, sometimes called framed modules, are designed to withstand all types of weather, including hail, snow, and extreme winds; manufac-

turers typically offer warranties of 20 to 25 years. Common module sizes range from about 2 ft. to 4 ft. in width and from 2 ft. to 6 ft. in length. Smaller modules often weigh less than 10 pounds, while large panels may be 30 to 50 pounds each.

In addition to variations in size, shape, wattage rating and other specifications, standard PV modules can be made with two different types of silicon cells. Monocrystalline cells contain a higher grade of silicon and offer the best efficiency of sunlight-to-electricity conversion, but are more difficult and expensive to make. Multicrystalline, or polycrystalline, cells are made with a less exacting and thus cheaper manufacturing process. Solar conversion of these is slightly less than that of monocrystalline cells, but warranties on panels may be comparable. All solar cells degrade slowly over time. Standard monocrystalline and multicrystalline cells typically lose 0.25% to 0.5% of their conversion efficiency each year.

Amorphous Solar Cells

Another group of solar products is made with amorphous, or thin-film, technology in which noncrystalline silicon is deposited onto substrates such as glass or stainless steel. Some substrates are flexible, allowing for a range of versatile products such as self-adhesive strips that can be rolled out and adhered to metal roofing, and thin solar modules that install just like traditional roof shingles. Amorphous modules typically offer lower efficiency—roughly half that of crystalline—and a somewhat faster degradation of 1% or more per year.

The Economics of Going Solar

While the environmental benefits of solar electricity are obvious and irrefutable, most people looking into adding a new solar system need to examine the personal financial implications of doing so.

Installing solar panels over an arbor, pergola, or other overhead structure can create a unique architectural element. Here, panels over an arbor provide shade for a patio space while generating electricity for the house.

This fiber-cement shingle roof features an integrated array of shingles laminated with thin-film PV modules.

PV systems cost only a small fraction of what they did 30 years ago, but they're still quite expensive. For example, a three-kilowatt system capable of supplying most or all of the electricity for a typical green home can easily cost $30,000 (before rebates and credits) and take 20 to 25 years to pay for itself in reduced energy bills. An off-the-grid system will cost even more. Nevertheless, depending on the many factors at play, going solar can be a sound investment with a potentially high rate of return.

One way to consider solar as an investment is to think of it as paying for a couple of decades' worth of electricity bills in advance. Thanks to the long warranties offered by manufacturers and the reliability of today's systems, the costs of mainte-nance on a system are predictably low. This means that most of your total expense goes toward the initial setup of the system. If you divide the setup cost (after rebates and credits) by the number of kilowatt hours (kWh) the system will produce over its estimated lifetime, you'll come up with a per-kWh price that you can compare against your current utility rate. Keep in mind that your solar rate, as it were, is locked in, while utility rates are almost certain to rise over the lifetime of your system.

Now, about those rebates and credits: In many areas, homeowners going solar can receive sizable rebates through state, local, or utility-sponsored programs, in addition to federal tax credits, as applicable. All told, these financial incentives can add up to 50% or more of the total setup cost of a new PV system. To find out about what incentives are available through any of these sources, check out the Database of State Incentives for Renewables & Efficiency at www.dsireusa.org. Established solar businesses in any given area are also very well informed about incentives available to local residents.

Here are some of the factors that tend to affect the cost of a PV system, its effectiveness or efficiency, and the homeowner's return on investment:

- The house and geographic location—how much sun reaches the house; the roof's slope and roofing material
- Electric utility rates and net-metering rates
- Increased home value—PV systems and other energy-saving upgrades can increase a home's resale value (often without raising the property value used for tax assessment)
- Loan rate, if the system is financed

Being off the grid means no electric bill, no concerns about rate hikes, and no utility-based power outages.

With so many factors to consider, getting to the bottom line can be complicated. Full-service solar companies will perform a cost/benefit analysis to help potential customers make a decision based on the financial picture. Of course, you should always check their numbers and scrutinize any variables used. You can also learn a lot by talking to other homeowners in your area who have had similar systems installed. Are they getting the return they expected? Have their systems been reliable and low-maintenance? Would they change anything if given the chance to do it over?

Working with Solar Professionals

Companies that provide solar equipment and system design, installation, and maintenance services are rising in number every year. A few of these were around during the lean years of the 1980s and 90s, but many more have sprouted up in the last decade or so. In any case, this is now a highly competitive industry, so you can, and should, expect great service at competitive prices.

The reputation and reliability of your local solar provider are important considerations, but perhaps more important is the stability of the original equipment manufacturers (OEMs) who produce the main parts of your system and who carry those long warranties. Many of these are large, well-established companies with expertise in energy and/or electronics, so it's a good bet they'll be around in 20 or 25 years to honor their product warranties. Always discuss warranties carefully with your solar provider.

Professional installation may run you around 15% of the total system cost—quite a low rate for the home improvement industry—and that amount is subject to rebates and credits, which are based on installed system prices.

Before giving you a quote for the system package, a solar provider will want to know about your home, what type of roofing you have, and what the southern exposure is like. To ballpark the size of system you'll need, they'll probably look at your utility bills from the past year and ask how much power you want to get from solar: Will it cover all household demand or just a portion of it? You may have to pay a fee to cover the provider's legwork required for working up an accurate quote.

Services likely to be included in a provider's system package are:

- Complete system design and installation
- Guarantees on workmanship/installation
- Obtaining building/electrical permits
- Coordinating hookup with utility company
- Obtaining rebates and credits
- Help with OEM warranty claims
- Lifetime technical support

Another thing to be aware of when comparing various providers' quotes, and in talking to other customers, is the actual output of a panel or array as opposed to its STC (or "name plate") wattage rating. Industry sources say the actual usable power of a system is typically about 75% of the rated power. This means that if your home needs three kilowatts of power your system should be rated for four kilowatts.

Solar Panel Safety

Solar panels and the various components they work with have a green, environmentally friendly feeling to them that makes it easy to let down your guard and forget normal safety rules. But remember that electricity from a solar panel can cause just as much damage as electricity from utility lines. Also remember that PV panels start generating electricity as soon as the light hits them, so cover them up or follow manufacturer safety recommendations until you're done installing.

First, always make sure you have necessary safety equipment like safety glasses, hardhats, work gloves and harnesses for roof work. Make sure you understand the electrical systems you're working on; if you're uncomfortable or confused, call an electrician to help out, or talk to the electrical inspector.

Any PV system that's big enough to provide power to a house needs charge controllers, fuses, inverters and circuit breakers (often both DC and AC). Full-service suppliers will provide complete systems with all the safety equipment, but if you're putting a system together on your own from discount components you bought on the internet, read up on the subject before you get started.

Solar panels have metal frames and must always be grounded, whether they're on the roof or a pole in the yard. Big metal objects outdoors can attract lightning strikes, and you need to be sure that if your array is hit, the energy will dissipate into the ground—not into your house.

Start by attaching 6-gauge bare copper wire to the metal frame of each PV panel with stainless steel bolts and star washers (or follow manufacturer recommendations). If the panels are on the house, connect the grounding wire to a separate ground rod and bond to the house grounding electrode system, either directly or through a grounding lug in the main circuit breaker box or a mechanical connection with the main ground wire. If the panels are on an outbuilding or a pole away from the house, you'll need to install a separate ground rod at that location. Use an 8-ft.-long solid copper ground rod ½" dia. or larger (sold at home centers), and pound it almost all the way into the ground, leaving just a few inches exposed. Attach the wire with a ground rod clamp. You'll also need to run 6-gauge wire underground back to the main house ground wire so all of your grounds are interconnected.

Check with your local electrical inspector about grounding recommendations in your area. If you live in an area with lots of lightning strikes, you may need to add additional grounding protection.

Wear a proper safety harness when working on a steep roof.

Lightning can strike anywhere, and solar panel arrays need to be properly grounded to protect them, and you, against damage.

Electricity from solar panels is just as dangerous as the kind that comes over the utility lines, especially for large, whole-house arrays. You may want to call in a pro to help with the final hookups.

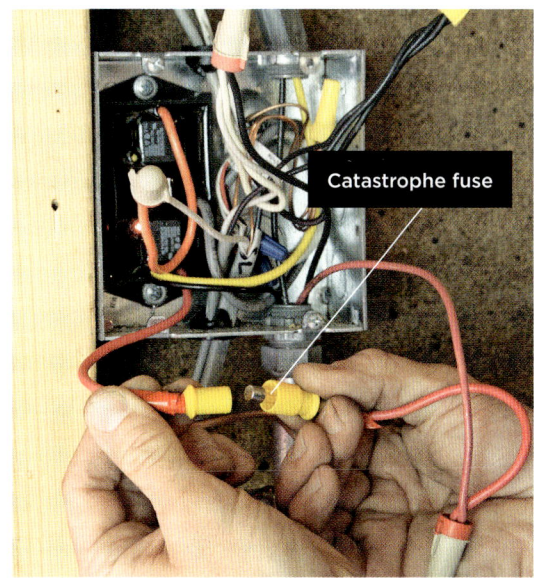

Catastrophe fuse

Remember to install all required fuses, charge controllers and circuit breakers to ensure the safety of the system and the people using it.

Applications for Solar Energy

Solar panel manufacturers have found a growing market for their products in countries that lack a reliable electrical grid.

A south-facing porch roof was added on to this house both for the solar panels and to make a cool outdoor sitting area.

The house is over a hundred years old, but the PV panels and the solar hot water collector in the background complement the architecture perfectly.

Silicon–From Raw Material to Solar Cell

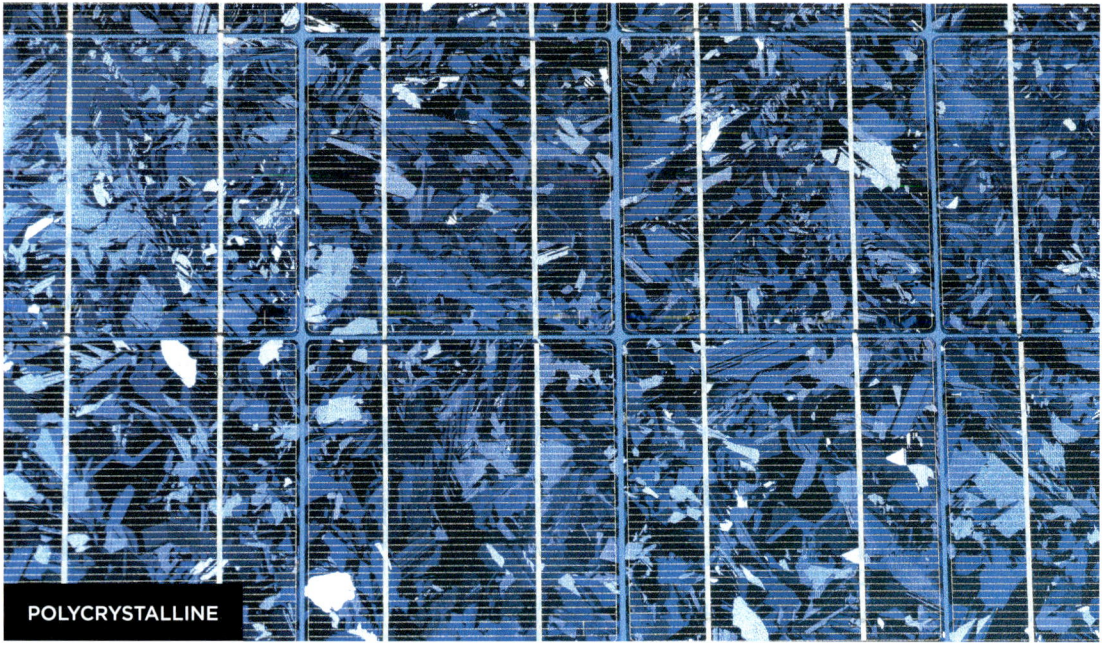

Photovoltaic panels made from polycrystalline silicon (top) have a visibly flaky appearance and are less expensive than monocrystalline cells (above). Both are covered by a panel of tempered glass in front and a plastic panel in the rear.

The initial investment required to be self-sufficient in energy is significant, but so is the reward of being able to live off-grid with all the modern comforts.

Two elements of an energy-efficient house: The photovoltaic panels provide most of the electricity, while the white roof reflects the sunlight and keeps the house cooler, substantially reducing energy demand.

Power and communications for a small village have been set up in an open field cleared in the jungle.

Assembling a Solar Electric System

Solar electric power is fascinating, exciting, and—as anyone who's browsed through the catalogs and websites can attest—kind of confusing. A solar panel wired directly to a fan or a light makes sense: sunlight is converted directly to power, much like the way sunlight is converted to heat. But as the solar panels get larger, you need fuses, charge controllers, inverters, system monitors, and other mysterious and expensive components that begin to turn the fascination and excitement of photovoltaics into a difficult homework assignment.

This extra equipment is required because solar panels produce DC power and store it in batteries, and that power must be regulated and controlled. The AC power coming from utility lines is not stored—it's generated and used on demand. DC power is different; it's all right there, sitting inside an innocent-looking battery like a caged lightning bolt, and if there's a problem like a short-circuit you can end up with melted wires, fried electronics and even fires.

To help visualize how it all works, we've put together a series of sample systems, starting with a basic panel powering a light and continuing up

to a whole house. We'll explain what you can do with different sizes of solar panels and what the add-on components are for—and why you need them. None of the pieces of a complete system are hard to understand once you know what they do, and you don't need to be an electrical engineer to put everything together. Any reputable, full-service supplier will make sure you have everything you need, including detailed instructions, and your local electrical inspector will also let you know if you're doing anything wrong (you generally need a permit for anything bigger than plug-and-play systems).

Photovoltaic systems start with a few simple connections, then grow in complexity with the size of the array. You don't need to understand all the components of a large system right away—just grab a small panel and aim it at the sun, and the rest will fall into place.

1. A Starter System with Low-Watt Panel

In this type of low-wattage system power flows directly from the solar panel to a DC motor, light, roof fan or battery. When the sun is out, the device works; as the sun goes down, the device slows down and finally stops. A low-wattage panel like this (less than 5 watts) can also be used to top off a 12V battery or keep a battery that's in storage charged during the winter, because the amount of power generated is low enough that there's no danger of overcharging.

Solar-powered garden lights are slightly more sophisticated because the panel charges a small rechargeable battery during the day instead of powering the light directly. The battery then powers the light when it gets dark.

Cell phone chargers are small and lightweight, and generally produce 5 watts or less of power. A basic solar panel like this doesn't store power—it will only charge the cell phone when the sun is out.

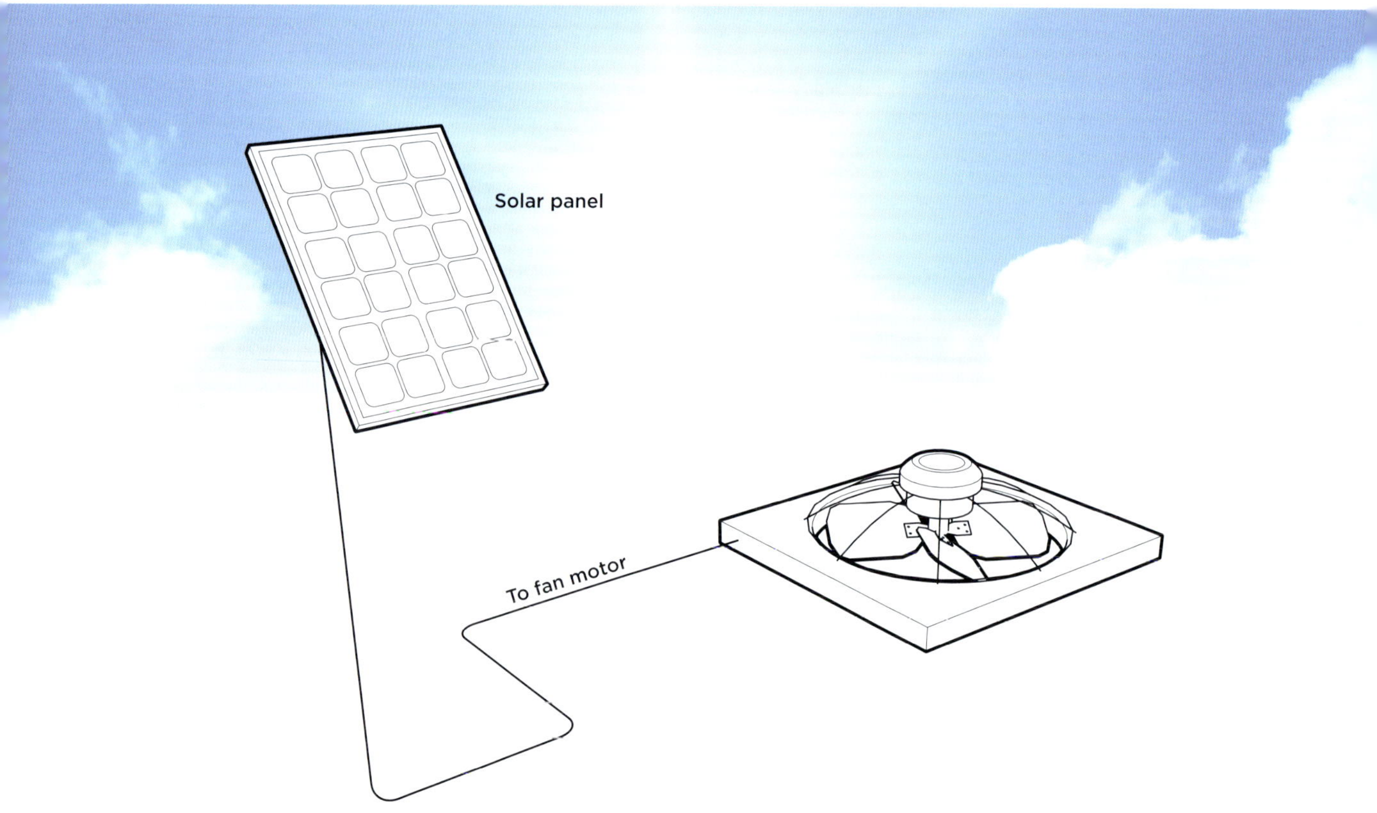

Solar panel

To fan motor

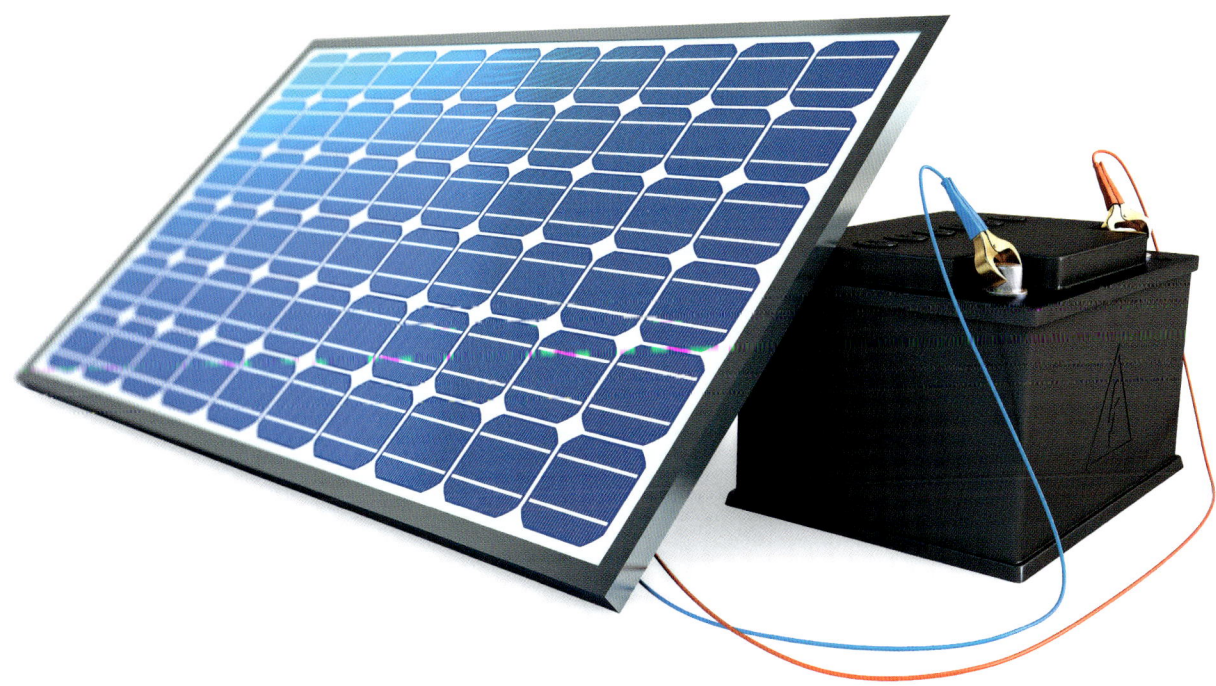

The essence of a photovoltaic system: A solar panel converts light to electric energy, which is used or stored in a battery.

A solar drip charger is connected to the terminals of a car, RV or boat battery to keep it fully charged when it is not in use for extended periods of time.

Portable, foldable solar panels are small enough to fit in a backpack or pocket, but have enough power to keep electronic gizmos charged up. You can even plug one into your car's cigarette lighter to top off the battery.

2. More Watts Equals More Power

As with the starter system, the DC motor in the pump used to refill this stock tank is powered directly by the solar panel, with no battery, and will not operate unless the sun is out. However, when the sun is out, the pump will operate more efficiently and produce more water than it would if the solar energy flowed through a battery, because up to a quarter of the energy generated by a solar panel can be lost when it is stored in a battery. The pump is given another boost by a linear current booster, which provides extra power to the pump when the light is low.

This type of system needs a larger panel to operate—typically 50 to 60 watts or more—and is usually sized by the solar panel dealer based on the well depth, pump size and other factors. It's the perfect system for the stock tank; the supply of water stockpiled in the tank on sunny days is more than enough for the demand, so no battery is needed. Roof vent fans, and pond pumps for water circulation and small fountains are other types of solar-powered fixtures that use power directly from the PV panels without a battery because they don't need to run at night.

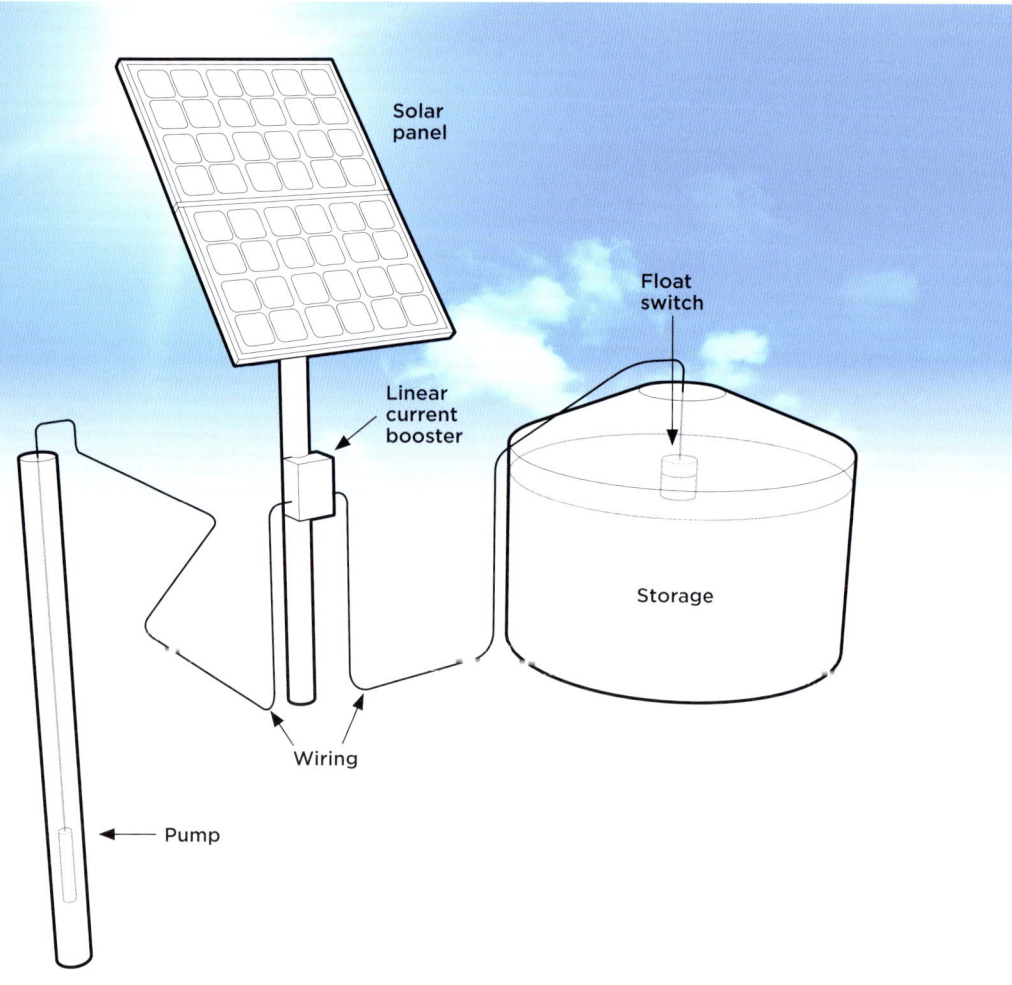

Solar
panel

Float
switch

Linear
current
booster

Storage

Wiring

Pump

Once powered by a windmill that needed frequent maintenance, this deep well, which pumps water to a nearby stock tank, is now powered directly by solar panels. Instead of pumping on demand, the motor pumps water continuously when the sun is out and stores it in a large tank.

Water for irrigation is continuously pumped from a deep acquifer up to this storage tank during the day as long as the sun is shining.

A solar-powered roof vent fan draws hot air from the attic during the day when the sun is out–the time when the attic is hottest. This type of fan generally does not include a battery, and is powered directly by the solar panel (although some manufacturers offer models with backup wind or AC power).

A multimeter is a good diagnostic tool for checking a photovoltaic panel to ensure it is working properly. It also allows you to check the power generated at different angles and locations.

3. Portable Power

This type of system begins to look more familiar, with a storage battery and a few AC outlets that can be used to power small appliances, electronics, lights, and even power tools. "Plug-and-play" type systems are generally under 100 watts, and are often small enough to be portable. Think of them as a silent alternative to a small gas-powered generator. They're useful for camping, emergency power, recreation, powering small garages and utility buildings and similar uses. You can find pre-packaged systems at suppliers, or you can assemble your own from the individual components. In this system several additional pieces of electrical equipment are added between the solar panel and the devices using the power:

- **Charge controller.** A charge controller regulates the amount of power going into the battery, and prevents the battery from being overcharged.

- **12V battery.** The battery stores energy collected when the sun is out, making power available at night.

A simple solar power system makes life in a yurt much easier. Inside the yurt a battery provides electricity for a few small appliances and a light.

- **Inverter.** The inverter converts DC (Direct Current) power coming from the battery into AC (Alternating Current) power, which is what most appliances and electronics use. Although DC appliances and lights are available, the selection is limited and often more expensive. However, DC appliances and lights don't require the inverter.

- **A small catastrophe fuse** is a safety feature, and is placed on the positive wire between the battery and the PV panel.

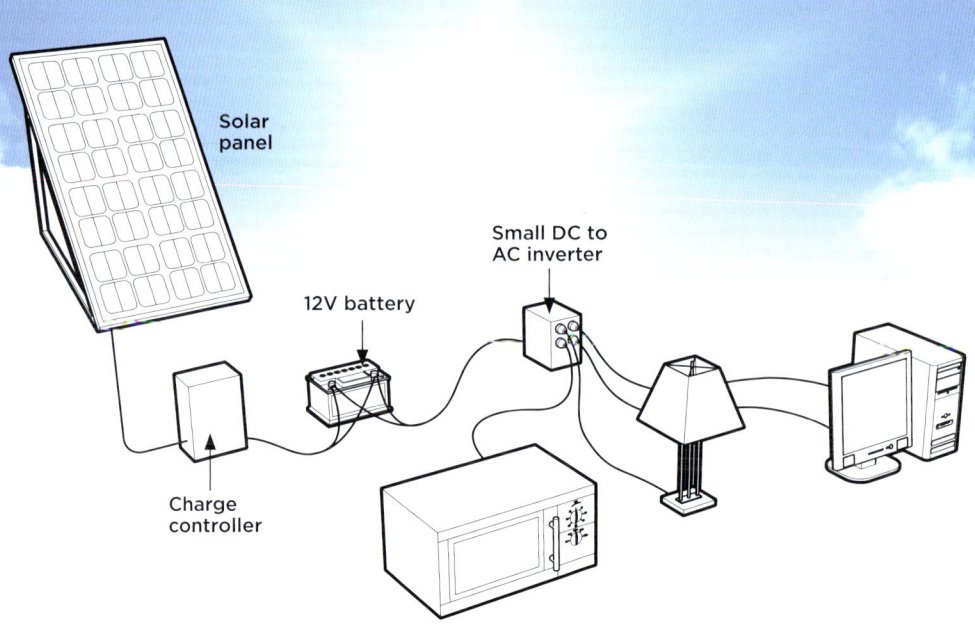

Solar panel

12V battery

Small DC to AC inverter

Charge controller

Solar power road signs are a common sight on highways. The light is plugged into a battery, which stores power produced by the PV panel. A charge controller keeps the battery from overcharging.

Buoy lights are a perfect use for a solar panel and battery. No other power source comes close to working as well and as cheaply for this application.

A solar panel and a small deep-cycle battery are a cleaner, quieter and lighter source of temporary power for a trip away from the power grid.

4. Off-Grid System for a Small Cabin or Weekend House

This system is large enough for a small, energy-efficient off-grid cabin or vacation home, providing power for lights, a well, electronics and a few basic appliances. If you do the installation and wiring yourself, the components for a system like this can be surprisingly affordable; some online dealers sell packages for $2,000 to $5,000. A small gas-powered generator or windmill can also be added to the system if needed for a backup power source during cloudy periods.

Larger houses or houses with lots of power-hungry appliances need additional solar panels and batteries, based on the size of the house, the power usage, location and other factors. Solar panel suppliers can help you size the system, and additional panels and batteries can be always be added in the future.

The additional components used in this system are:

- DC safety disconnect. The safety disconnect allows you to shut off the flow of power from the panels to the battery for maintenance or repairs.
- DC load center. The DC equivalent of a circuit-breaker box.

Although this back-country cabin only has a small number of panels, they generate power all week, providing plenty of energy for a cabin used only on weekends.

- AC circuit breaker. This is a small version of the circuit-breaker box found in almost every home.
- System monitor. A system monitor tracks power consumption and will let you know if your batteries are getting dangerously low (fully discharging a deep-cycle battery will shorten its life).

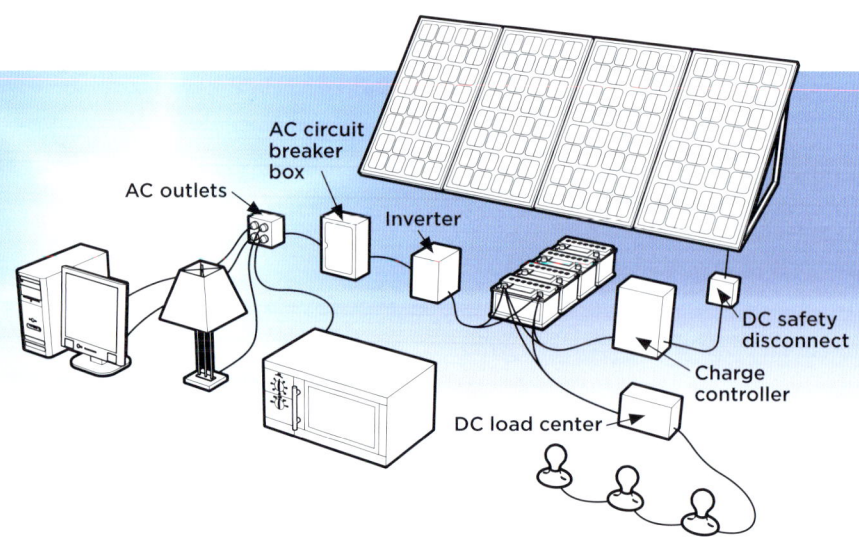

This small, energy-efficient modern house uses PV panels for power. Energy is conserved with energy-efficient appliances, extra insulation, a light-colored roof to deflect heat, and louver-shaded windows.

A camper van this size consumes as much energy as a small house, all of which would normally be generated by idling the motor. Although the large solar panels are a significant investment, they pay for themselves quickly in this desert campground, and they're also completely silent.

5. Whole House, Grid-Connected System

A whole-house system connected to the power grid will need an array of solar panels producing several thousand watts of power to meet household needs (depending on house size, energy efficiency and other factors), but the system is fairly straight-forward, especially if you dispense with the battery backup. Power flows to a grid-tied inverter designed to work with the utility-system electrical grid. The incoming DC power from the solar panels is converted to AC with an inverter, then fed into the house circuit-breaker box and used just like power from the utility company. Any power that's not needed flows into the electrical grid through a production meter, running the meter backwards. The electrical grid functions like a battery, absorbing extra power or providing it, as needed. If you create more power than you use, most utility companies will pay you or credit you for the excess.

One of the advantages of this type of system is that you can start small, then add additional solar

If your house already has power lines coming in from the utility company, it makes sense to leave them connected when you install solar panels so you can use the electrical grid for storage and backup.

panels later. It also eliminates the need for expensive batteries and ensures a continuous, reliable flow of power. However, if the utility company suffers a blackout, the solar panels will not be able to provide power to the house unless you have a battery backup system in place.

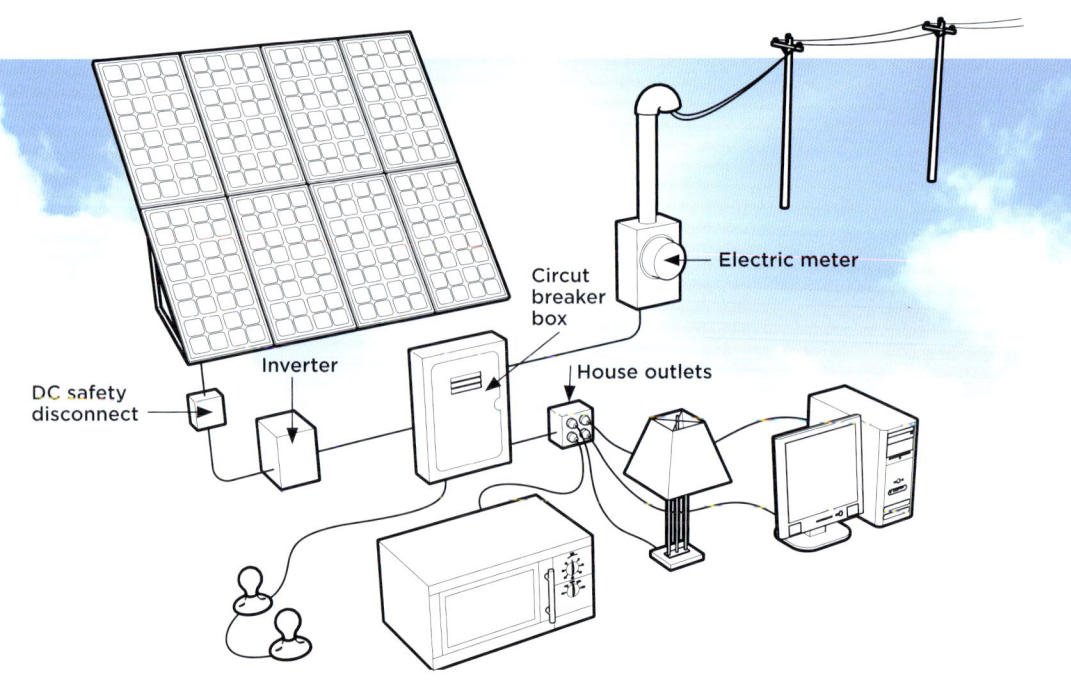

ABOVE: This house is still connected to the electrical grid, but with the entire south side of the roof covered with solar panels, the homeowner generates enough electricity on sunny days to earn money back from the utility company.

LEFT: Power generated by wind or water supplements solar-generated power, providing an alternative source of power at night or in cloudy weather. It can also be wired to the same grid-tied system that the solar panels are connected to.

BATTERIES

Charging batteries with power from a solar panel is simple and straightforward. There's no need for an inverter to change the DC power produced by the panel to AC, since batteries store power in DC form (it's not possible to store AC power in batteries). Chargers are available for any size or type of rechargeable battery, including batteries in computers, cell phones, cameras and other electronic devices. Small rechargeable batteries (AAA through 9V) are sold most places where regular batteries are sold, and can be used anywhere standard batteries are used. Nowdays most are nickel-metal hydride (NiMH), which are less toxic than nickel-cadmium (NiCad) batteries. Small, portable solar chargers that can charge all the different sizes are available at internet sites that sell solar products (see Resources, p. 136).

Charging the larger 6-, 12- and 24-volt batteries used for off-grid and backup power can get a little more complicated, with unique maintenance and use requirements. If you're interested in setting up an off-grid system, talk to an expert or the people who sell the solar equipment about recommended batteries. Large battery assemblies for off-grid living are expensive, and if they're not properly maintained they can fail quickly.

Solar power can be used to recharge any size or type of battery, as long as it's a rechargeable type.

A FEW IMPORTANT POINTS TO REMEMBER ABOUT BATTERIES

Batteries sold for cars are designed to pump out a lot of power quickly, but will rapidly break down if used for long periods of low power output, so they can't be used for an off-grid power source. However, they can still be charged with PV panels.

Always buy "deep-cycle" batteries for storing solar power. Deep-cycle batteries can safely discharge most (but not all!) of the power stored in them between charges. The least expensive deep-cycle batteries are marine types; the most expensive are those sold for industrial applications. Life expectancy runs from 2 to 25 years, with prices based on life expectancy. It's a good idea to start with marine batteries, then work up to the expensive, longer-lasting types.

Batteries used for both cars and off-grid power storage are lead-acid types. Newer battery technologies like nickel-metal hydride (NiMH) are still too expensive for large battery arrays, though this could change soon.

Solar charging a battery, no matter what size, always takes longer than charging the same battery from a standard AC outlet. Depending on what you're charging and how low the battery is, it could take several hours to several days.

Lead-acid batteries are available as either "wet cells" or sealed cells. Wet-cell batteries have removable caps and must be refilled with distilled water periodically. Sealed cells are permanently sealed and never need refilling, but they're more expensive and need to be charged at a lower voltage than wet cells.

Always use charge controllers between the solar panel and the battery, unless the solar panel is a small (5 watts or less) trickle-charging type just used to top off the battery when it's in storage.

Large batteries need fuses between the solar panel and the battery and circuit breakers or fuse boxes between the battery and appliance or fixture. (Note that systems for houses can be purchased with all electrical and safety components preassembled into one unit. See Resources, p. 136).

With the proper charge controllers and wiring, deep-cycle batteries will accept power from several different sources. These two solar panels and small fan provide just enough power for the electronics and lights on this sailboat.

Solar chargers for small electronics generally have a small battery inside that builds up power for charging when you leave it out in the sun.

Mounting Solar Panels

Mounting solar panels so that they'll stay in place through weather, high winds and ground movement for 25 years or more is probably the most demanding part of any installation. With so much surface area the panels can catch gusts of wind almost as well as a sail. They also need to hold up against rain, seasonal movement, snow loads, hail and whatever else nature throws against them. They must be securely mounted and well-anchored to the roof, ground, or side of the house with rust-resistant metal poles and rack systems, and the best stainless-steel hardware, and they should be checked periodically for loose fasteners.

Although home-built solar water and heat collectors can be mounted on wood posts on the ground, solar PV panels have a longer life expectancy and are best mounted on steel or aluminum supports that can hold up to the weather indefinitely, especially up on a roof. If the panels are roof-mounted, the condition of the roof should also be evaluated before they're installed. The panels can last 20 to 25 years or more, and if the roof is going to need replacement before then it's best to do it before installing the panels so you can avoid the expense of removing and reinstalling the panels later.

Needless to say, it's important that the panels face the sun as directly as possible and get at least six hours per day—without shading—year-round. Spend some time on research and observation before you proceed with installation to avoid putting up panels that only get sufficient sun for half the year.

Solar panel dealers can recommend mounting systems for the panels they sell, but the following pages will give you a basic overview, along with some ideas for a simple mounting system you can build yourself.

The large surface area of solar panels means that they must be very securely mounted to resist the force of the wind.

To protect them against damage due to frost heave and ground movement, solar arrays must be set on posts that go down to frost-footing depth, or at least 2 ft. When using treated lumber, let it dry out for several weeks before using it so it doesn't warp or shrink under the panel.

Mounting thin-film solar panels can sometimes be as simple as gluing them to a metal roof. Thin-film solar panels aren't as efficient as standard solar panels in full light, but they perform better in low-light conditions. They're also flexible, cheaper to manufacture and more versatile.

Ground-Mounted Panels and Collectors

Assuming your solar panel or collector works as it should, it will be mounted outdoors on your house or in your yard for many years. The supports holding it need to be the best quality and materials possible.

Ground-mounted photovoltaic panels are generally attached to galvanized steel poles set deeply into the ground and anchored in concrete, with the depth of the hole, the amount of concrete and the size of the steel post determined by the square footage and height of the PV panel. For example, a single 3 ft. × 5 ft. (15 s.f.) panel set five feet above the ground should be mounted on a 2½" Schedule 40 steel post (sold at home centers) and set into the ground at least 3 ft. (or to frost-footing depth in your area) in a 12"-diameter hole filled with concrete. However, if four of the panels are mounted together in an array (60 s.f.), you'd need to use a 4" post (actual 4½" O.D.), and set it a minimum of 4 ft. down in a 20- to 24"-diameter hole. If the panel is higher than five feet, you'll need to make the hole 6" deeper for every extra foot of height. Local soil and wind conditions may also necessitate a larger or deeper hole—it's best to get specific guidelines for your area and panels from your dealer or building inspector.

Solar water or hot air collectors can be mounted on pressure-treated posts buried in the ground or attached to post bases, or fastened to steel U-channel supports. In either case the posts should be anchored or set in concrete below the frost level, just as posts for a deck would be, or set 2 ft. down if freezing is not a consideration.

Collectors or panels are also occasionally mounted to the side of a house, but they must be securely fastened to the studs with galvanized lag bolts. Mounting to the side of an aluminum- or vinyl-sided house should be a last-ditch option though, as the large holes created by the lag bolts are difficult

PV panels are often installed on heavy metal pole mounts, embedded in a cylinder of concrete and buried deep in the ground. The size and depth of the post mount for a PV panel is based on the square footage of the panel or panels, the height above the ground and local soil and wind conditions. You also need to take into account snow levels and the furthest reach of shadows cast by nearby trees and buildings throughout the year.

or impossible to repair if the collector is ever removed, unless you have pieces of the original siding.

Manufactured solar hot water heaters should be mounted according to manufacturer recommendations.

Always select a location for the solar panel that faces south and gets at least six hours of unshaded sun year-round. If possible, mark the furthest extent of shadows from nearby trees and buildings during the winter, because winter shadows will be substantially longer than summer shadows when the sun is higher overhead. If you can't wait until winter, consult a local dealer or installer for rough guidelines, or check online for shadow calculators (see Resources, p. 136). Also remember to set the panel high enough so it's well above the possible snow level in the winter.

The mounting system used for this solar hot water collector straddles the ridge of the roof so that the panels will face due south even though the house faces east/west.

Mounting solar panels does not always have to be a complicated job.

These molded supports for solar hot water panels are set at 45°—a safe, compromise angle for year-round use in most of the country. The wide base of the supports distributes the weight of the panels evenly on the flat roof.

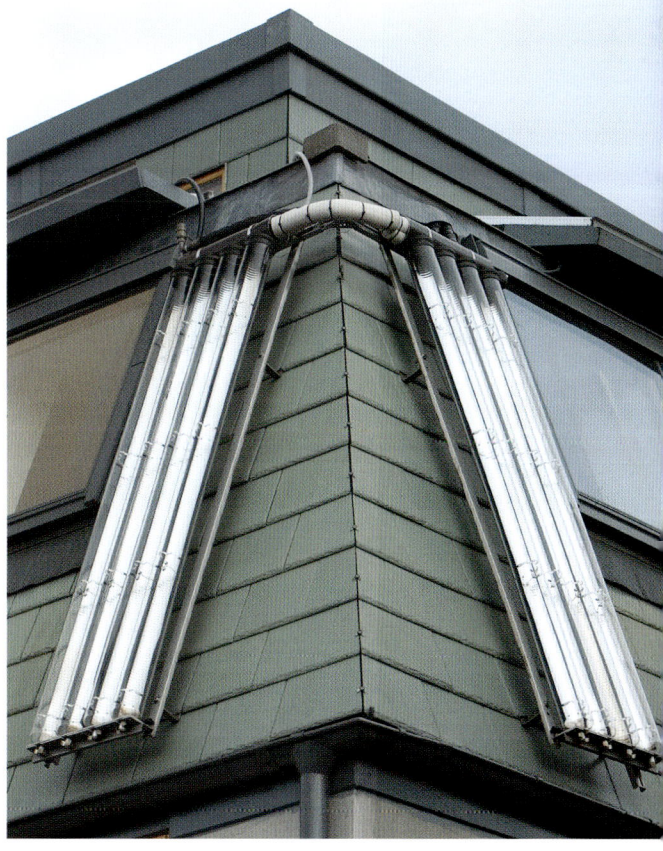

An unusual roof style and a NE/SW building orientation called for a creative mounting solution for this evacuated-tube solar hot water collector.

A ROOF OR GROUND SUPPORT FOR SOLAR PANELS

You can make a sturdy support for either PV panels or solar collectors by assembling lengths of Unistrut U-channel (sold at home centers and electrical suppliers; see Resources, p. 136) and then anchoring them to the roof or ground. Use galvanized or stainless-steel pieces and fasteners, and follow the same guidelines for selecting a location and height.

Struts are available in several sizes, with a huge selection of accessories for joining them in dozens of configurations, though you may have to go online to find them. With a little hunting, you can usually find the right combination for almost any location or roof layout. We made ours from the basic accessories sold in the local home center, but the basic design can be put together in any number of ways with other types of fittings and fasteners.

A few considerations to keep in mind: Solar panels or hot water heaters placed on a roof need to be bolted to the rafters every 4 to 6 ft. with stainless-steel or triple-galvanized lag bolts (at least $\frac{5}{16}$ x 4"). These holes need to be waterproofed with extra care, as they will be difficult to get to once the panels are up.

Build a simple, adjustable support from steel U-channel struts (above) for either solar panels or the solar hot water collector (inset).

CUTTING LIST

Part / Number	Dimensions
Base (2)	80"
Support (2)	92"
Back brace (2)	36"
Brace expanders (4)	20"
Cross braces (4)	48" (or to fit)

TOOLS & MATERIALS

Adjustable wrench

Socket set

Metal-cutting saw

1⅝" × 10' Galvanized Unistrut (if exterior-grade galvanized is unavailable, paint the metal)

1⅝" × 3½" Unistrut angle brackets

1⅝ × 3½ Unistrut flat corner brackets

⅜" × 1½" bolts and Unistrut spring-loaded nuts

½" × 1½" bolts, nuts, washers

Speed Square

Hinges or L-bracket

Concrete mix

(2 or 4) Anchor bolts

Gravel

First of all, the collector should face directly south and should not be shaded, although the location doesn't have to be perfect. Crystalline solar cells should not be shaded at any part for at least six hours because shading even a small part will diminish the energy collected by the whole array, but this is not as much of a problem for thin-film solar cells or solar collectors. Solar panels and collectors are often put on roofs to elevate them above trees and shade from buildings, but they work just as well on the ground or attached to the side of a building as long as they have sufficient sunlight.

The best tilt angle is not necessarily the same for PV panels and solar collectors. For either one, though, start by finding your latitude (check online for latitude finders). The best angle for a PV panel is the same degree as your latitude, though for maximum efficiency you can move it 10° more in the winter and 10° less in the summer. For example, at latitude 45 you would put it at 55° (from horizontal) in the winter, 45° in the spring and fall, and 35° in the summer.

For a solar collector, on the other hand, add 15° to your latitude. For example, if you live at latitude 45, the tilt angle is 60° from horizontal. Use your speed square, which has angle markings on the outer edge, to mark this angle, then just adjust the supports for the collector until it matches the angle. This angle is generally the best for both winter and summer, because it faces the sun more directly in winter, but not as directly in summer, which lessens the chance of overheating; if you can't match it exactly, several degrees either way won't have much of an effect.

If you're mounting the support on a sloped roof, use the speed square to lay out the angles and determine the length of the back brace. Angles and roof pitch are both marked on the square; just align the base strut with the common rafter cut mark corresponding to your roof pitch, then align the PV support strut with the degree mark for your latitude. For example, if your roof slopes 4" in every 12" (a 4/12 pitch), the base strut will follow a line from the pivot point through the number 4 on the "Common Cuts" edge. The other strut follows the line from the pivot through the 45° mark on the outside edge.

However, these are not absolute rules. Following the slope of your roof will usually be close enough to the ideal that you won't notice much difference. And it's always a good idea to talk to local dealers, installers or homeowners who have solar panels for advice about local conditions.

Solar panel dealers carry various options for flashing roof mounts (see Resources, p. 136). For shingled roofs, these are usually a bracket or holder bolted to the rafter and then covered by flashing, a rubber boot, rubber seals or some combination of these elements, with the upper part of the flashing slipped under the shingle above the holder. These mounts are the safest option when you're installing solar panels, as they've been tested and carry a manufacturer's warranty.

(continued)

How to Make a Roof or Ground Support for Solar Panels

1 The easiest way to figure out the strut lengths is to lay the three pieces on the ground, move the support piece to the proper angle using the angle markings on the speed square as a guide, then mark the cuts. Use tape to mark the location of the solar collector or panels and the points where the adjustable support leg will be attached.

2 Cut the pieces to length. Cut the cross supports to match the width of the solar collector or the length between mounting points on the PV panels.

3 Cut two additional pieces of strut to 4″ less than the length of the expandable brace. Cut the expandable brace in half, then bolt both halves to the long center leg with four bolts. To expand the brace to the fall or winter position, just remove the bolts on one side, push the frame up, and then bolt the pieces back together. (Note that solar collectors usually stay in a fixed position year round, while PV panels benefit from being moved to summer and winter positions.)

Bolt the brackets and struts together, but don't join the two sides yet. Join the pieces at the base with hinges, or just use an L-bracket with a bolt as the pivot, as we did.

Although the PV mount is stable, it needs to be securely anchored to the ground in case of high winds. For larger arrays like ours, add concrete footings at each corner.

Stand-Alone Solar Light System

One of the easiest ways to put photovoltaic panels to work around your home is to purchase a self-contained kit. Kit contents and qualities vary, and if you apply the dollars–per–watt cost calculations most pro installers use, kits aren't the best value. But it's a very user-friendly way to jump into solar. If you have a garage or shed on the far reaches of your property and you'd like to convert it to useful work space where you can store and charge batteries, watch TV or play music, or just put in some overhead lighting for hobby work, a kit like the one shown here may be just the answer you're looking for.

The kit used in this project is a 45-watt, 3-panel PV kit purchased from a large discounter. In addition to the three 15-watt PV panels, it includes two 12-volt lights, battery hookups, a combination regulator/charge controller/safety fuse, and an adapter plug for different DC appliances. To complete the installation, the only missing elements are a roof boot to seal the roof penetration for the panel wires (if you come through the roof) and electrical conduit for the wire leads from the panels. You'll need enough conduit to get from the back of the panels to just above the regulator/charge controller.

You can set this up as a battery charging station for car, boat and RV batteries, or you can just install a permanent deep-cycle battery and use it to power a few lights and DC chargers and appliances. You can also use the system to power AC appliances and lights, but you'll need to add a power inverter with a minimum capacity of 300 watts.

The PV panels slip into angled mounting brackets that can be placed either on a flat surface or a pitched roof. If you are working on a pitched roof, follow all safety precautions for working at heights and wear fall-arresting gear if the pitch is steep.

With the PV panels and a charge controller in place, this solar power generating station can do a lot more than just charge batteries, even without an AC inverter. Use it to supply power to a pond or waterfall pump, add a few DC lights, hook up garden lights, or just keep a few deep-cycle batteries charged up for emergency power in case the utility lines go down in a storm. If you live in the frozen north, it's also the perfect power source for an ice-fishing shack. Just plug in a DC-powered light, coffee maker and TV and you're good to go.

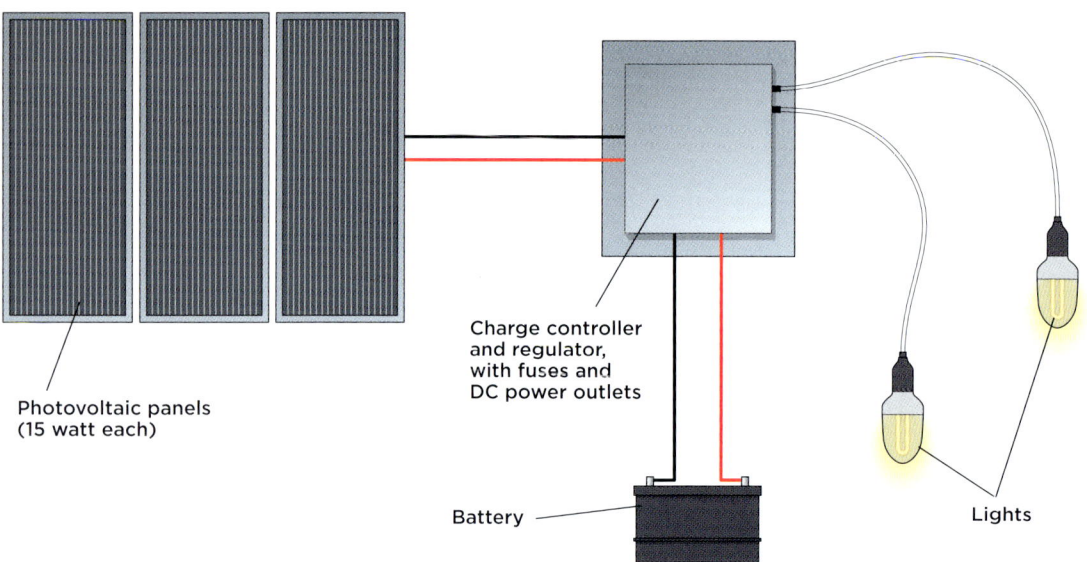

Photovoltaic panels
(15 watt each)

Charge controller
and regulator,
with fuses and
DC power outlets

Battery

Lights

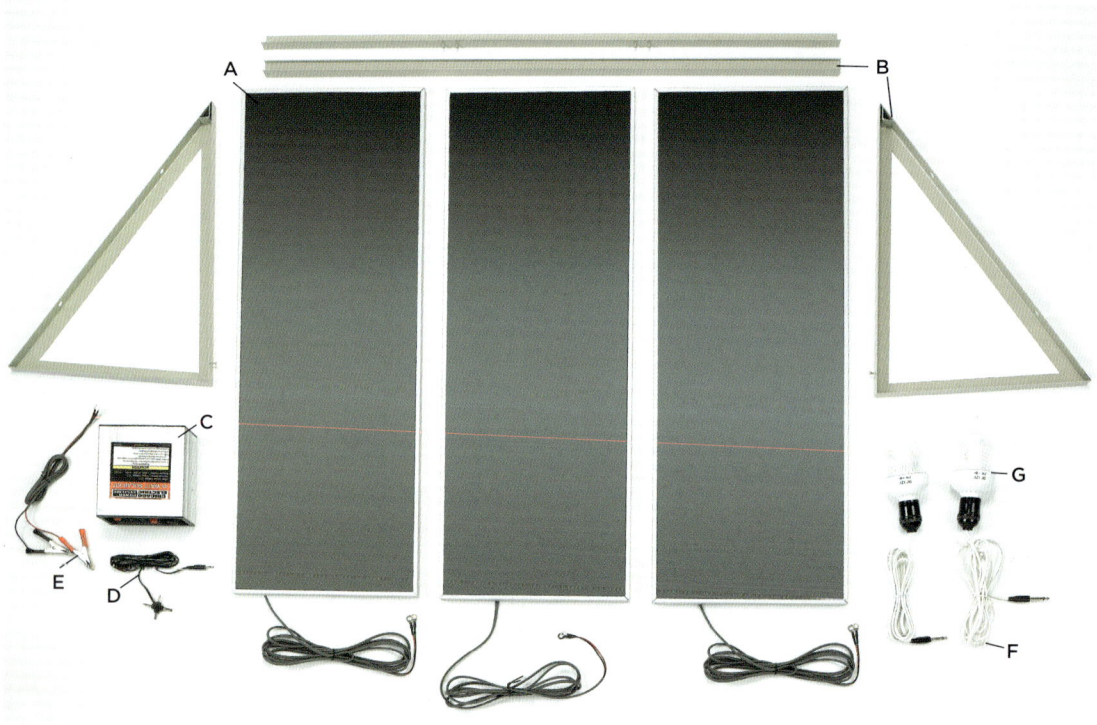

Parts of this solar light kit include: Three 15-watt photovoltaic panels (A); snap-in mounting stand (B); regulator (C); multi-purpose adapter (D); battery connectors (F); light wires (F); 12-volt LED lights (G). A 12-volt battery is required but not included with the kit.

How to Make a Solar Light System

1 Predrill the holes for the mounting brackets after locating the roof rafters, either by using a stud finder or by lifting up shingle tabs and tapping in finish nails. You must plan to fasten at least one of the angled mounting brackets to a rafter. If the other doesn't fall on a rafter, plan to attach it with toggle bolt anchors.

2 Fill the holes for the mounting brackets with roofing cement or silicone caulk. Fasten the brackets to the roof with neoprene screws (small lag screws with a rubber washer), or with toggle bolts if not attaching to a rafter.

3 Fit the bottom of the first collector panel neatly into the slot in the mounting frame assembly.

(continued)

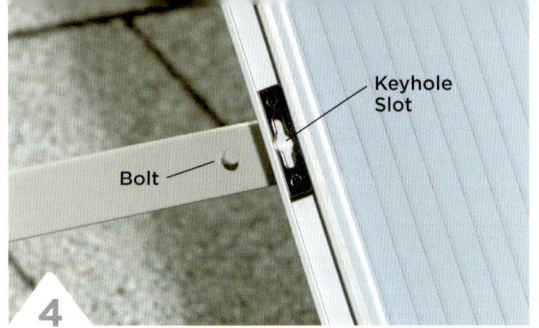

4

Lock the PV panel down into position by sliding the small bolt heads on the brackets into the keyhole slots on the back of the panel. (Other kits may use different fasteners.) Cover the panels with a drop cloth after they're in position—they'll start generating electricity as soon as the sun hits them.

5

Check the underside of the roof for electrical lines or ductwork. Locate an access hole for the panel cable into the roof deck, directly behind the panel assembly. Buy a flashing boot with a rubber boot sized for small electrical conduit (¾" or 1" is best–check online or at electrical or roofing suppliers if you have difficulty finding one). Place the boot so that the top edge extends under two shingle tabs, then drill a test hole with a ¼" bit. Leave the bit in place and double-check the underside of the roof to make sure you come out in the right spot. If everything looks good, finish the hole with a hole saw or spade bit big enough for the conduit to fit through.

6

Cut a piece of conduit long enough to go through the roof and extend several inches above the boot. The conduit should continue on the underside of the roof over to the location of the regulator. Push the pipe through and hold it in place with a pipe strap or block of wood. Slip the roof boot over the pipe and wiggle it into place under the shingles. Spread roofing cement or silicone under the sides (but not the bottom) of the metal flashing, then nail it to the roof. Glue a 90° elbow to the conduit, turning it downhill, and extend with more conduit (if necessary) to the back of the PV assembly. Fish the leads from the panels through the conduit to the regulator; you may need to use an electrician's fish tape for this job. Finally, plug the opening in the conduit around the wires with electrician's putty or caulk to seal out bugs and drafts.

7

Install two sturdy shelves inside the building to hold the regulator and the battery. The shelf should be easily reachable by an adult so the equipment can be turned on and off and plugged into the adapter easily. The battery shelf should be at least 18" off the ground.

8

Connect the wires from the PV panels to the solar terminals on the back of the regulator/charge controller. Secure the wires to the walls or roof framing members to keep them clear. *CAUTION: The collector panels should be covered with a drop cloth or opaque material well before making these connections. Tape or clamp the drop cloth so it doesn't blow off.*

9

With the regulator turned off, fasten the battery leads to the back of the regulator, then clamp them to the battery posts–black to negative first, then red to positive. Then uncover the PV panels. Double-check the connections, then turn the regulator/charge controller on. For a 12V battery, the voltage output reader (inset) will show 13 when the battery is fully charged.

10

This kit includes two DC lights. To install them (or other DC appliances), just plug the cord in to the proper port (or adapter) and turn the power on. Hang the 12-volt light fixtures from the rafters and then staple the cords to keep them secure and out of the way. Make sure to leave enough cord that the plug end is easy to insert and remove from the port. You'll plug and unplug the lights to turn them on and off.

Solar-Powered Security Light

A self-contained electrical circuit with dedicated loads—usually 12-volt light fixtures—is one of the most useful solar amenities you can install. A standalone system is not tied into your power grid, which greatly reduces the hazards involved in installing the components yourself. Plus, the fact that your light fixtures are independent of the main power source means that even during a power outage you will have functioning emergency and security lights.

Installing a single solar-powered circuit is relatively simple, but don't take the dangers for granted. Your work will require permits and inspections in most jurisdictions, and you can't expect to pass if the work is not done to the exact specifications required.

Solar panels can be small and designed to accomplish a specific task, or they can be large enough to provide power or supplementary power to an entire house. Before you make the leap into a large system, it's a good idea to familiarize yourself with the

mechanics of solar power. The small system demonstrated in this project is relatively simple, and is a great first step into the world of solar. The fact that the collector, battery, and lights are a stand-alone system makes this a very easy project to complete. By contrast, installing panels that provide direct supplementary power through your main electrical service panel is a difficult wiring job that should be done by professional electricians only.

This 60-watt solar panel is mounted on a garage roof and powers a self-contained home security lighting system. Not only does this save energy costs, it keeps the security lights working even during power outages.

TOOLS & MATERIALS

Tape measure

Drill/driver with bits

Caulk gun

Wiring tools

Metal-cutting saw

Socket wrench

Photovoltaic panel (50 to 80 watts)

Charge controller

Catastrophe fuse

Battery sized for 3-day autonomy

Battery case

Battery cables

12-volt LED lights including motion-sensor light

Additional 12-volt light fixtures as desired

20 ft. Unistrut 1⅞"-thick U-channel (see Resources, p. 136)

45° Unistrut connectors

90° Unistrut angle brackets

Unistrut hold-down clamps

⅜" spring nuts

⅜"-dia. × 1"-long hex-head bolts with washers

Green ground screws

DC-rated disconnect or double throw snap switch

6" length of ½"-dia. liquid-tight flexible metallic conduit

½" liquid-tight connectors

Lay-in grounding lugs

Insulated terminal bars to accept one 2-gauge wire and four 12-gauge wires

Cord cap connectors for ½"-dia. cable

½" ground rod and clamp

Copper wire (6- and 12-gauge)

Square boxes with covers

½" flexible metallic conduit or Greenfield

½" Greenfield connectors

11⁄16" junction boxes with covers

PVC 6 × 6" junction box with cover

14/2 UF wire

¼ × 20 nuts and bolts with lock washers

Roof flashing boot

Roof cement

Silicone caulk

Eye protection

Schematic Diagram for an Off-the-Grid Solar Lighting System

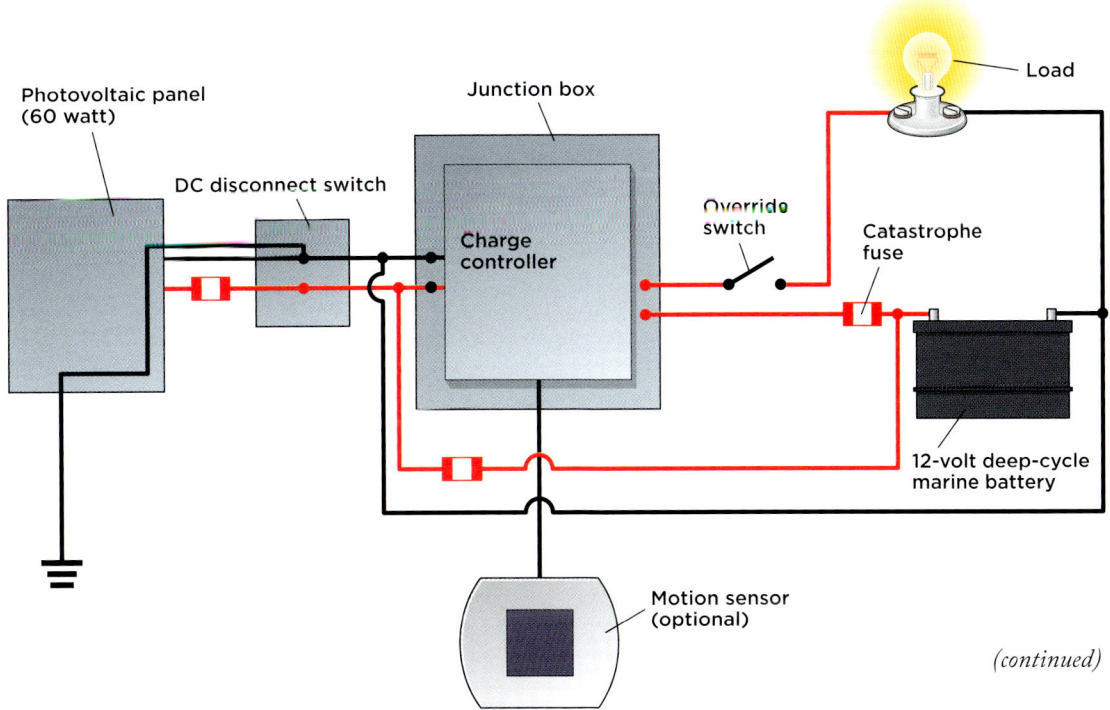

(continued)

Mounting PV Panels

The mounting stand for the PV panel is constructed from metal U-channel and pre-bent fasteners (a product called Unistrut is seen here. See Resources, p. 136). Position the solar panel where it will receive the greatest amount of sunlight for the longest period of time each day—typically the south-facing side of a roof or wall. For a circuit with a battery reserve that powers two to four 12-volt lights, a collection panel rated between 40 and 80 watts of output should suffice. These panels can range from $200 to $600 in price, depending on the output and the overall quality.

The stand components are held together with bolts and spring-loaded fasteners. The 45° and 90° connectors are manufactured specifically for use with this Unistrut system.

Connections for the feed wires that carry current from the collector are made inside an electrical box mounted on the back of the collector panel.

An EPDM rubber boot seals off the opening where the PVC conduit carrying the feed wires penetrates the roof.

How to Wire a DC Lighting Circuit

1 Mount a junction box inside the building where the conduit and wiring enter from the power source. Secure the box to the conduit with appropriate connectors. Run two 14 gauge wires through the conduit and connect them to the positive and negative terminals on the panel.

2 Plan the system layout. Determine the placement of the battery and then decide where you will position the charge controller and DC disconnect. The battery should be placed at least 18″ off the ground in a well-ventilated area where it won't be agitated by everyday activity. Mark locations directly on the wall.

3 Attach a junction box for enclosing the DC disconnect, which is a heavy-duty switch, to a wall stud near the battery and charge controller location. Use a metal single-gang box with mounting flanges.

4 Run flexible metal conduit from the entry point at the power source to the junction box for the DC disconnect box. Use hangers rated for flexible conduit.

(continued)

5 Attach a double-gang metal junction box to the building's frame beneath the DC disconnect box to enclose the charge controller.

6 Attach the DC disconnect switch to the wire leads from the power source.

7 Install the charge controller inside the double-gang box. Run flexible conduit with connectors and conductors from the disconnect box and to the charge controller box.

8 Mount a PVC junction box for the battery controller about 2 ft. above the battery location and install two insulated terminal bars within the box.

9 Build a support shelf for the battery using 2 × 4s. The shelf should be at least 18" above ground. Set the battery on the shelf in a sturdy plastic case.

10 Set up grounding protection. Pound an 8-ft.-long, ½"-dia. ground rod into the ground outside the building, about 1 ft. from the wall on the opposite side of the charge controller. Leave about 2" of the rod sticking out of the ground. Attach a ground rod clamp to the top of the rod. Drill a ⁵⁄₁₆" hole through the garage wall (underneath a shake or siding piece) and run the #6-gauge THWN wire to the ground rod. This ground will facilitate lightning protection.

11 Wire the DC disconnect. Attach the two #14-gauge wires to the two terminals labeled "line" on the top of the DC disconnect switch.

12 Run wiring to the loads (exterior DC lighting fixtures in this case) from the charge controller. DC light fixtures (12-volt) with LED bulbs can be purchased at marine and RV stores if you can't find them in your home center or electrical supply store.

(continued)

OPTION: Attach a motion sensor. Some charge controllers come equipped with a motion sensor to maximize the efficiency of your lighting system—these are especially effective when used with security lighting. The motion sensor is typically mounted to a bell box outside and wired directly to the charge controller with an 18-gauge × 3-conductor insulated cable. A system like this can support up to three motion sensors. Follow the manufacturer's directions for installing and wiring the motion sensor.

14 Install the battery. Here, a deep-cycle 12-volt marine battery is used. First, cut and strip each of the two battery cables at one end and install into the battery control junction box through cord cap connectors. Terminate these wires on two separate, firmly mounted insulated terminal blocks.

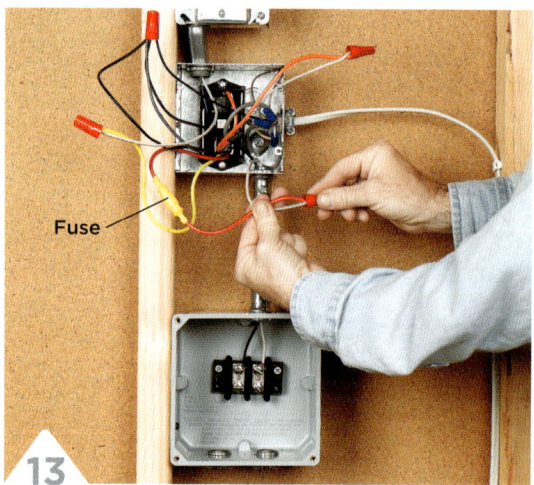

Fuse

13 Wire the charge controller. Route two more #14-gauge wires from the bottom of the DC disconnect terminals into the 4 × ¹¹⁄₁₆ junction box and connect to the "Solar Panel In" terminals on the charge controller. The black wire should connect to the negative terminal in the PVC box and the red to the positive lead on the charge controller. Finish wiring of the charge controller according to the line diagram provided with the type of controller purchased. Generally the load wires connect to the orange lead and the red wire gets tied to the battery through a fuse.

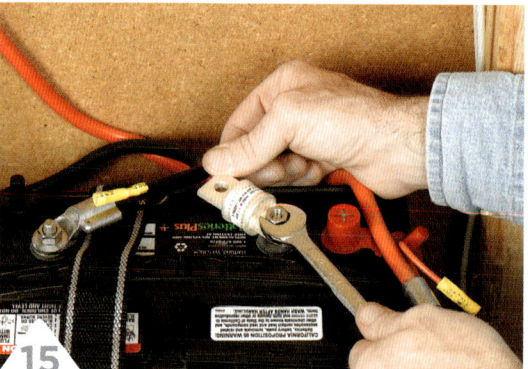

15 Install the catastrophe fuse onto the positive terminal using nuts and bolts provided with the battery cables. Connect the battery cables to the battery while paying close attention to the polarity (red to positive and black to negative). Make sure all connections have been made and double checked.

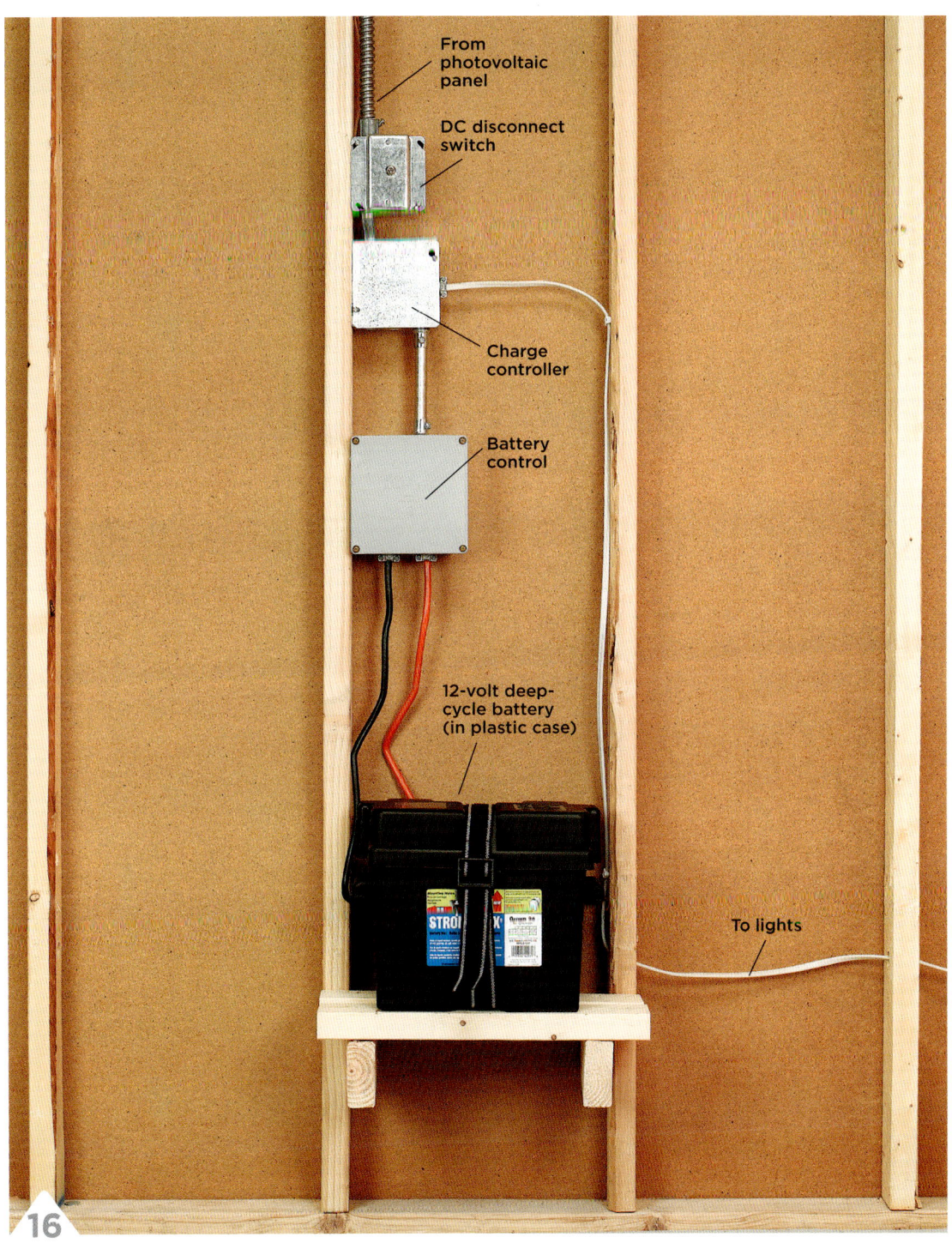

From photovoltaic panel

DC disconnect switch

Charge controller

Battery control

12-volt deep-cycle battery (in plastic case)

To lights

16

Cover all junction boxes, then remove the bag from the panel and turn the DC disconnect switch on to complete the circuit. Test the lights and adjust the time to desired setting.

Solar Heat

Unlike photovoltaic panels, solar collectors are everywhere around us. In fact, we're living in one. The Earth itself is one giant collector, absorbing light from the sun and keeping just enough of it under an insulating layer of atmosphere for life to exist.

Solar collectors work in a similar way, and although the scientific explanation for what they do is complicated, actually making one is not that difficult. There are basically two ways to collect solar heat and put it to a useful purpose, and we'll show projects that illustrate each type. The first is probably the simplest and most familiar, especially if you've ever owned a car with a black interior and left it parked in the sun with the windows rolled up. Dark colors absorb heat, and if they're in a space covered with glass much of the heat will be trapped, then come blasting out when you open the door. That's the principle behind the solar hot air collector on page 109. Solar hot water collectors take the idea a step further, by transferring that stored heat to water flowing through heat-absorbing pipes (see p. 85), after which it can be used for hot water or heat throughout the house, or even stored for later use (p. 109).

The second method is a little different. Instead of just absorbing heat in a black box, solar energy is first concentrated and focused by a reflective surface. This can be a curved, highly polished array of mirrors capable of generating heat measuring in the thousands of degrees, or it can be reflective foil glued to the slanting sides of a box, bouncing enough solar heat towards a black pot to cook a chicken dinner (p. 75).

Either way, solar heat collectors have one big advantage over PV panels— a faster return on your investment, especially if you make your own.

IN THIS CHAPTER

A large array of solar hot water collectors makes a significant dent in the hot water bill at this mountainside resort.

Collecting the Heat of the Sun

If you ever burned a dry leaf with a magnifying glass when you were a kid, you've harnessed the power of the sun with a solar collector. Solar collectors are fascinating, but unlike PV panels are really pretty easy to understand—a very powerful but very accessible technology.

Solar collectors convert sunlight into heat, even in the dead of winter, then use that heat to do useful work: cook food, heat water or air, or even generate electricity by creating steam to power a turbine. You don't need to understand physics to make a good solar collector; you just need to have an understanding of how to collect and use heat.

This gallery of solar heat collectors illustrates a few of the possibilities—all working, proven technologies. Many others are available, and most will work well whether you live near the equator or the North Pole, or anywhere else the sun shines.

The evacuated-tube hot water collectors mounted to the side of this house in the desert collect abundant hot water for bathing and heat. Evacuated tubes are well-enough insulated that they can survive an occasional cold snap.

In this thermosyphon hot water collector, heated water rises into the storage tank at the top and then flows into the house as needed. This simple system is widely used in warmer parts of the world where freezing temperatures are not a problem.

The ability of a magnifying glass to concentrate solar heat enough to start a fire has been known since at least 700 BCE. Solar collectors that concentrate sunlight use the same basic principle.

This solar collector uses parabolic reflectors to heat oil passing through a pipe to 750°F. This hot fluid is then used to boil water and generate steam, which powers turbines that create electricity. This power plant has been in operation since 1985.

Uses for Solar Heat

Instead of using expensive fossil fuels to heat the water in this pool, the homeowners installed solar hot water collectors to utilize the free heat of the sun.

Solar panels and collectors can be fastened to corrugated metal roofs without expensive standoff systems, since rainwater just drains underneath.

Cool water enters these flat-plate hot water collectors at the bottom, then gradually rises to the top as it is heated. A pump then moves it to a storage tank inside the house.

It looks like some strange metal bird, but it's actually a solar cooker boiling water for tea. The panel is shaped so that all the reflected sunlight is focused on the base of the pot.

OPPOSITE: Under the right conditions—sunny climate, high energy prices, political support—solar hot water collectors can catch on fast. Notice all the black rectangular collectors on the roofs in this city on the Mediterranean coast of Turkey.

ABOVE: Arrays of hot water collectors are ganged together at the top and bottom. Cool water flows in at the lower right at one end of the array, and heated water flows out at the upper left. This system is controlled by a pump inside the house.

Hot water collectors are often mounted almost vertically to capture more of the winter sun and less of the summer. Collectors can actually get too hot if the water sits for a long period. The PV panels on the roof, however, need all the sun they can get.

Drainback solar hot water systems are safe for year-round use, even in cold climates. Water is pumped to the collectors only when the temperature in the collector is higher than the temperature in the storage tank, so there's no danger of freezing pipes.

For peak performance, clean dirt and leaves off solar panels and solar collectors. If your collectors are up on a sloped roof, spraying with a hose from the ground will do the job.

Solar Oven

Solar ovens are simple devices that capture heat from the sun with a reflective surface that's angled or curved towards a cooking pot. Because they can be easily made from cheap materials like scrap cardboard and tinfoil, they are widely used in areas of the world where trees and fossil fuel are scarce or expensive. Once made, they can be used to cook food and boil water in a reasonable amount of time for absolutely no cost.

There are dozens of possible designs (see Resources, p. 136); some angle the rays down into a small center area, while others focus the rays upward toward the underside of a pot, like a reversed magnifying glass. You can also buy portable solar ovens assembled from polished metal online—they're great equipment for camping. But if you're serious about integrating free fuel from the sun into your cooking, the plan on pages 78-83 features a solar oven that works beautifully and is also built to last. Plus, you can build it for a fraction of the cost of a purchased solar cooker.

Depending on variables like location, ambient air temperature and the angle of the sun, a solar oven can reach temperatures above boiling (212°F). In ideal conditions, some types can reach 300°F or more. This temperature range is high enough that you can safely cook any food, including meat. Cooking times are longer, but because the temperature is lower there's little danger of overcooking, and the food is delicious.

Solar Oven Types

Solar cookers can be made in a wide variety of designs. The main criteria is that they have a reflective side or sides that focus sunlight toward a heat-absorbing (usually black) pot or base.

Made from cardboard and aluminum foil, this solar cooker is still capable of heating food almost to boiling. Variations of this basic design are widely used in poor areas of the world that have abundant sunlight but limited fuel; their use helps preserve dwindling forests.

You don't need charcoal for an outdoor grill—just open up your solar cooker and turn on the sunlight.

In a dry, arid region of Tibet with little available firewood, a homeowner uses this ingenious solar cooker to heat water and cook food.

Take this solar cooker on picnics and camping trips. The angled blades focus light on the pot in the center, then fold up into a compact bundle when you're done.

SOLAR OVEN

There are numerous ways to make a solar cooker—one website devoted to the subject has dozens of photos of different types sent in by people from all around the world—and all of them seem to work reasonably well. We settled on this model mostly because we're carpenters and we like working with wood more than metal. Feel free to modify it as you wish.

The cooker is big enough to hold two medium-size pots. All the pieces are cut from one eight-foot-long 2 × 12 and a sheet of ¾" plywood. The cooker would work just as well with ¼" plywood, but we used ¾" because it made it simpler to screw the corners and edges together. The base is made from 1½"-thick lumber for ease of construction and for the insulation value of the thicker wood, but thinner material would also work.

The foil we used was a type recommended for durability and resistance to UV degradation by an independent research institute. Unfortunately, it was expensive, and if you're just starting out you may want to do a trial run with heavy-duty aluminum foil. Although foil looks a little dull, it actually reflects solar rays almost as well as specially polished mirrors.

TOOLS & MATERIALS

Straightedge

Circular saw

Jigsaw or plunge router

Tape measure

Drill/driver with bits

Speed square

Stapler

Eye and ear protection

#8 countersink bit

¾" × 4 × 8-ft. BC or better plywood

2 × 12 × 8-ft. SPF SolaReflex foil (see Resources, p. 136) or heavy-duty aluminum foil

1⅝ and 2½" deck screws

Clear silicone caulk

Contact cement, or white glue and brush, optional

Mid-size black metal pot with glass top

Wire rack

¼ × 17¼ × 17¼" tempered glass

No-bore glass lid pulls (Rockler item no. 29132)

¼ × 2" hanger bolts with large fender washers and wingnuts

CUTTING LIST

KEY / PART / NUMBER	DIMENSION	MATERIAL
A Base (2)	1½ × 11¼ × 19"	SPF
B Base (2)	1½ × 11¼ × 16"	SPF
C Bottom (1)	¾ × 19 × 19"	Plywood
D Adjustable leg (1)	¾ × 10 × 17"	Plywood
E Back (1)	¾ × 20 × 33¾"	Plywood
F Front (1)	¾ × 10 × 25¼"	Plywood
G Sides (2)	¾ × 20 × 31¼"	Plywood
H Cover (1)	¼ × 17¼ × 17¼"	Tempered glass

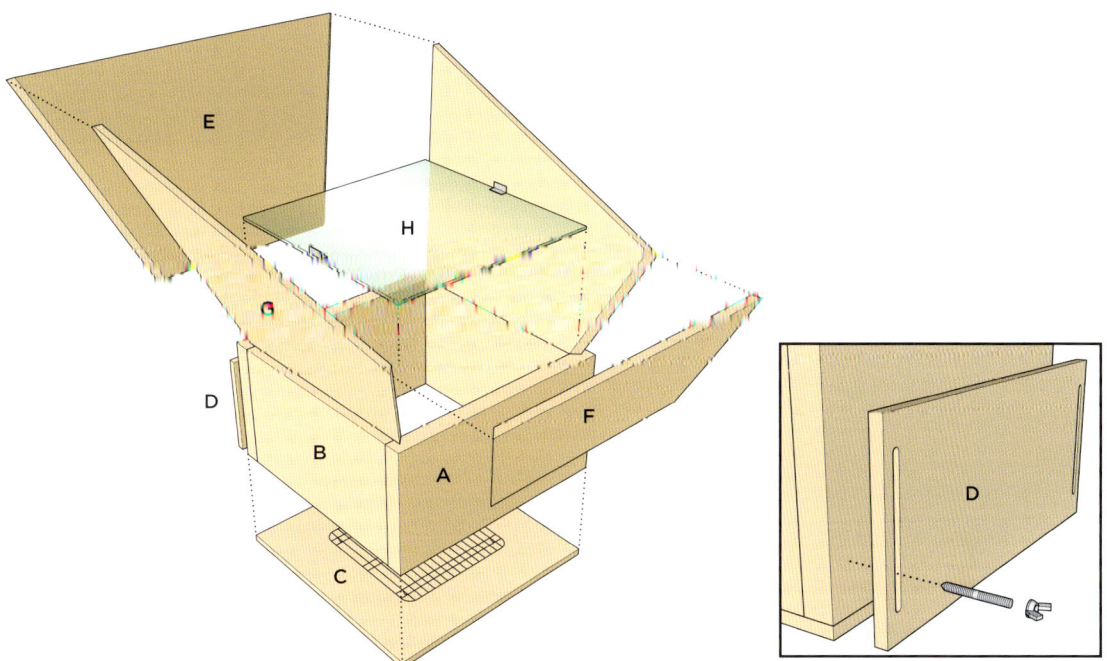

Sun rays reflect off the foil sides and are concentrated at the base of the cooker, where they are absorbed by the black pot. The glass cover (or clear oven cooking bag) helps hold heat and moisture in the pot. The cooker should face the sun. Raise or lower the box depending on the time of year so that you catch the sun straight on. Shim the wire rack as needed to keep the pot level.

How to Build a Solar Oven

Cut the four 2 × 12 base pieces to length according to the cutting list. Arrange the base parts on a flat work surface and clamp them together in the correct orientation. Check with a carpenter's square and adjust the parts as needed. Then drill pilot holes and fasten the pieces together with 2½" deck screws.

Lay a 4 × 8-ft. sheet of plywood on the work surface with the better side facing up. Select a good grade of ¾" plywood (we used BC) or you're likely to have issues with parts warping, and you'll find it difficult to drive screws into the edge grain of the plywood. Mark and cut the 19 × 19" bottom piece first. Rest the full sheet of plywood on a couple of old 2 × 4s—you can cut through them as you make your cuts without any need to move them out of the way.

(continued)

COMPOUND MITER CORNER CUTS

The sides of this solar cooker box are cut with the same basic technique used to cut crown molding. Instead of angling the crown against the miter saw fence in the same position it will be against the ceiling—a simple 45° cut that is easy to visualize—you have to make the compound cuts with the wood lying flat, which makes it mind-bendingly difficult to visualize the cut angles. For the dimensions of this cooker, a 40° bevel cut along the 22½° line will form a square corner. If you change the 22½° angle, the saw cut will also change.

If you remember your geometry you can work all this out on paper, but bevel guides on circular saws are not very precise, and 40° on one saw might be more like 39° on a different brand; test cuts are the best way to get the angle right. Make the first cuts a little long and then try them out.

The easiest way to avoid a miscut is to lay all the pieces out with the bases lined up and the good side of the plywood up. Mark the 22½° lines for the sides, then cut the 40° angles on one edge of all four pieces. Next, flip the piece around and cut the 40° angle on the other side. Remember, the 40° cut should angle outwards from the good side of the plywood, and the pieces should all be mirror images.

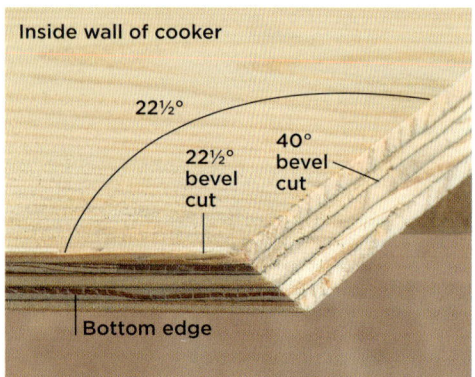

Inside wall of cooker

22½°

22½° bevel cut

40° bevel cut

Bottom edge

76" — 20"

3

To create the panels that form the reflector you'll need to make beveled cuts on the bottom and sides so the panels fit together squarely. With the best side of the plywood facing up, mark two 20" x 76" long pieces, measuring from the two factory edges so the waste will be in the middle. Set your circular saw base to 22½°, then cut along the line you drew at 20" (20" is the long side of the bevel). Cut the other piece starting from the opposite end of the plywood. You should end up with two mirror image pieces.

Centerline

8"

22½°

4

Re-set your saw base so it's flat, then cut each 20"-wide panel in half so you have four 20 x 38" panels, each with one beveled 38" edge. With the beveled edge facing up and closest to you, draw a centerline at 18" on each panel, then make marks on the beveled edges at 8" on both sides of the centerline. Position a speed square so it pivots at the 8" mark, then rotate the speed square away from the centerline until the 22½° mark on the speed square meets the top of the beveled edge. Draw a line along the speed square as shown, then use a straightedge to extend the line to the other edge (the factory edge) of the plywood. Repeat at the other 8" mark, flipping the speed square and rotating it away from the centerline so the lines create a flat-topped triangle. Set the base of your circular saw at 40°, then cut along the angled lines (although it seems incorrect, 40° is the angle required to form a square corner when the pieces are assembled). Mark and cut the remaining three panels in the same fashion.

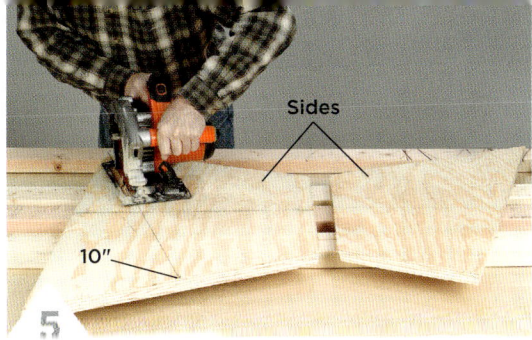

5 Finish cutting the reflector parts to final size and shape. TIP: Clamping or holding smaller parts for cutting can be tricky. Here is a useful trick: After you've laid out your cutting lines, set the workpiece onto a pair of old 2 × 4s. Tack the workpieces to the 2 × 4s with finish nails, ideally driven into the waste area of the panels. Keep the nails at least a couple of inches from any cutting line. Set your saw so the cutting depth is about ¼" more than the thickness of the workpiece and then make your cuts.

6 Assemble the reflector. Brace two of the reflector sides against a square piece of scrap plywood clamped to the work surface, then join the edges with screws driven into countersunk pilot holes. Repeat for the other two pieces, then join the two halves together with four screws at each corner, completing the reflector. The bottom edges should be aligned. The top edges won't match perfectly, so sand them smooth.

7 Make the adjustable leg, which contains parallel slots so the leg can move up and down over a pair of hanger bolts, raising and lowering the angle of the cooker so you can take full advantage of the direction of the sun's rays. Outline the slots in the adjustable leg of the oven so they are ⅜" wide (or slightly wider than your hanger bolt shafts). Locate a slot 2" from each edge of the adjustable leg. The slots should stop and start 2" from the top and bottom edges. Cut the slots with a jigsaw or a plunge router.

8 Screw the base and the plywood bottom together. Set the adjustable leg against one side of the base, then drill guide holes and install the hanger bolts so they will align with the slots. The centers of the bolts should be at the same height: roughly 2½" up from the bottom of the box. Use large fender washers and wingnuts to lock the adjustable leg in position.

(continued)

9

Fasten the reflector to the base with countersunk 2½" screws. Angle the drill bit slightly as you drill to avoid breaking the plywood edge. Use two screws per side.

10

Cut pieces of reflective sheeting to fit the sides of the reflector as well as the base. You can use heavy-duty aluminum foil, but for a sturdier option try solar foil (see Resources, p. 136). The product seen here is essentially polyethylene tarp material with a reflective aluminum surface. Make sure to cut the pieces large enough so they overlap the edges and can be easily attached.

11

Glue the reflective sheeting inside the base and reflector, overlapping the corners so all bare wood is covered. Use contact cement or silicone caulk to adhere solar foil, and staple the edges to reinforce the glue; use diluted white glue with a paint brush instead of contact cement if you're using aluminum foil. Pull or smooth out the reflective material as much as possible; the smoother the surface is, the better it will reflect light.

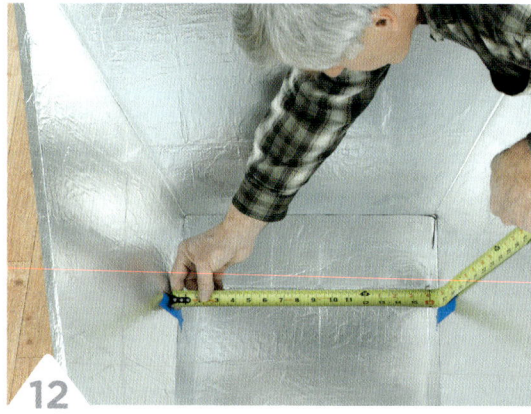

12

Take measurements to double-check the glass lid size. Ideally, the lid will fit in so it comes to rest about 1" above the top opening of the box. As shown here, a ¼ × 17 × 17" piece of tempered glass fits just right. Be sure to order glass with polished edges. You can also just use a clear plastic oven bag instead of the glass. Either will trap heat and speed up the cooking.

Caulk the joint between the angled top and the base with clear, 100% silicone caulk. Set a wire rack inside the oven to keep the cooking pot slightly elevated and allow airflow beneath it.

COOKING WITH A SOLAR COOKER

Anything that can be cooked in a slow cooker, including meat, can be cooked in a solar cooker (as long as the sun is out!). You can also make bread and other baked goods, rice, fish, potatoes, and dozens of other dishes. You'll need to experiment a little with a cooking thermometer, because cooking times will vary depending on the time of year and where you live; most foods will need 2 to 4 hours. Other points to keep in mind when cooking in a solar oven:

- Be sure to adjust the back leg so there are no shadows in the cooker, and move the cooker every hour or so to face the sun directly.

- Since the cooking temperature is fairly low and the food is in a closed pot, it won't over-cook or dry out if you leave it in too long.

- You can use a candy thermometer or oven thermometer to find out how hot the oven is. This will help you determine cooking time.

- Avoid opening the lid unless absolutely necessary—it's estimated that every time you open the lid you add 15 minutes to the cooking time.

- Wipe down the interior of the oven after every usage. Keeping the glass lid clean allows as much sunlight in as possible.

- You cannot cook in the oven without a dark pot with a lid. The dark metal of the pot is warmed by the sunlight and transfers its heat to the food.

- See the Resources section (p. 136) for links to sites with solar cooking recipes.

- Do not allow children to use the solar oven unless they are under direct adult supervision.

HANDLING FOIL

If you use rugged solar foil to create the reflective surface, you can glue it to the 2 x 12s and the plywood base prior to assembly. If you are using heavy-duty aluminum foil, which tears easily, you'll get better results if you glue it to the wood surfaces after the box is assembled.

GETTING A HANDLE ON GLASS

Since it is virtually impossible to lift the glass lid from above, you'll need to install handles or pulls designed to attach to glass (available from woodworking hardware suppliers) to lift and replace the glass cover. The simplest of these (see Resources, p. 136) require no drilling. You squeeze a bead of clear, 100% silicone into the U-channel of the lid handle, then slide the handle over the edge of the glass.

Solar Water Heater

The basic principle of a solar water heater is simple. Water or an antifreeze solution flows through pipes in a large, flat, enclosed box known as a flat plate collector, or through a series of vacuum tubes in an array known as an evacuated-tube collector. As the liquid moves through the system, solar heat is transferred to it. In a thermosyphon system, the solar-heated water flows into a storage tank and is used directly. In a drainback system, the solar-heated liquid— which can be water or antifreeze solution—flows into a heat exchanger inside a water-storage tank, where it heats potable water; the solar-heated liquid is not used directly.

Storing the hot water in a separate tank is necessary because it takes longer for the water to heat up, and because a large supply is needed to last through the night and early morning. Solar water heaters are usually paired with a conventional gas or electric water heater—either a tank or a tankless, point-of-use type—to ensure uninterrupted hot water during cloudy periods or times of heavy use, but the conventional heater won't turn on unless it's needed, which saves considerable money. And solar hot water heaters work anytime the sun is out, even in winter.

A number of different manufactured hot water collectors are available, but you can build your own for a fraction of the cost using wood, copper pipe and polycarbonate glazing—all materials available at home centers. The concept is simple, and can be modified to fit your house and needs. There are also many alternative designs available on the internet (see Resources, p. 136).

Hot water collectors can serve a number of different purposes. If you have enough sun, they can provide all the hot water for your household, but even on cloudy days the water will warm up enough to reduce the amount of energy you need. Using them with tankless heaters saves even more money, eliminating the need to keep a conventional water tank full of expensively heated water all day and night. Hot water collectors can also be used to provide heat for pools and hot tubs, and to heat water for use in a heating system.

This attractive solar heater array provides hot water for two families.

Solar Water Heater Types

The supports for this solar hot water collector are angled at 45°—a reasonable compromise between the ideal summer and winter angles.

Thermosyphon hot water heaters work without pumps or controls. Heated water flows into the upper part of the storage tank, which draws cooler water from the bottom of the storage tank into the bottom inlet of the storage collector. The water is part of the house system, so whenever the hot water faucet is turned on, hot water flows out of the storage tank and fresh cold water flows in.

This type of thermosyphon system uses evacuated-tube hot water collectors and an attached storage tank at the top to provide hot water. It works well in both a tropical climate (top photo) and a cool northern climate.

COPPER TUBING HEATER PANEL

This flat plate collector can be used with several different types of solar hot water systems. In warm climates it can work with a thermosyphon storage tank (see p. 96); in cooler climates where freezing is a problem it can be used as a rooftop or wall collector with a drainback system (see p. 98), or other type of pump-controlled system. It's also possible to use this collector with a system containing antifreeze, but water heaters with antifreeze require special plumbing and safety features to avoid contaminating the water supply, and should be discussed with a plumbing inspector or left to an expert.

The collector is constructed of wood with a layer of insulation to help retain heat. The panel covering it is made from polycarbonate, a type of clear acrylic that resists the UV damage that clouds and cracks regular acrylic. Cool water comes in through a ¾" pipe at the bottom and is gradually heated as it rises through a manifold of ½" copper pipes. Heat is collected and transferred to the pipes by thin aluminum panels lining the box and shaped over the copper. As the water warms in the pipes, it rises to the top and flows into the upper part of the storage tank as cool water from the bottom of the storage tank flows in to replace it. This water movement continues until the water in the storage tank is hotter than the water in the collector, at which point the thermosyphon action stops or the thermostatically-controlled pump switches off.

The collector can be mounted on the ground (as we did—see p. 42), the roof, or the side of the building, at an angle based on the latitude (see p. 43). However, these collectors can get quite hot during the summer months, and they are often placed at a steeper angle so that they face the low winter sun more directly, and deflect some of the intense heat from the high summer sun.

If you can solder pipe and cut wood, you can build a collector like this, and start saving money on water heating costs right away.

Use polyisocyanurate rigid insulation (usually called "polyiso") for the insulation in a solar collector as it has the highest R-value and is also the most heat-resistant type of rigid insulation. Polyiso has a variety of trade names; just look for the insulation with the highest R-value.

To simplify construction, the size of this collector is based on a sheet of plywood, but it can be built a different size or orientation or ganged together with other collectors to make a larger array. Deciding how big a collector you need is mostly trial and error based on your usage and climate, but the square footage of a sheet of plywood is a good starting point for an average household. If it's not enough, you can always add another one.

TOOLS & MATERIALS

Level

Circular saw

Miter saw

Tape measure

Drill/driver with bits

Stapler

Razor knife

Soldering torch

Wire brush for copper pipe

Adjustable wrenches

Hammer

½" plywood

½" × 4' × 8' plywood

¾" rigid Polyisocyanurate insulation

¼" plywood 2 × 4 × 8' for sides, bottom; 2 × 6 × 51" for top

Copper tubing cutter

Sledgehammer

⅝" steel rod

High-temperature black paint

PEX crimping tool

¾" × ¾" inside nailers, nailers for glazing, caps for top and bottom

¾" × 1½" top nailer for glazing

½" × 40½" EMT cross supports for glazing

Neoprene rubber screws

1¼", 1⅝", 2½" deck screws

¾" machine screws

½" machine screws

6d galv. casing nails

Aluminum soffit panels

Aluminum coil stock

Paintable acrylic caulk

Clear silicone caulk

Polycarbonate glazing (¼" × 2 × 8' panels)

Closure strips (sold with glazing)

Stainless-steel staples

Emery cloth

¾ × ½" Ts

¾ × ¾" T

¾ × ½" elbows

¾" elbow

¾" male threaded coupling

¾" cap

¾" hose bibb

½ × 85½" Type L copper

16 copper tubing cut to fit (pieces between Ts)

(2) 10" long × ¾" (inlet and outlet)

(2) ¾ × ¾ PEX adapters

¾" PEX tubing (to inside house)

¾" pipe wrap insulation

Lead-free solder

Paste flux

Teflon tape

Copper pipe straps

EMT conduits

½ and ¾" type L copper tubing

Copper fittings

Hose bibb

PEX tubing

PEX to copper transitions

Copper soldering supplies

¾" pipe wrap insulation

(continued)

CUTTING LIST

KEY / PART / NUMBER	DIMENSION	MATERIAL
A Top (1)	1½" × 5½" × 48"	PT or SPF
B Sides (2)	1½" × 3½" × 95"	SPF
C Bottom (1)	1½" × 3½" × 45"	SPF
D Underside (1)	¼" × 45" × 93½"	Plywood
E Nailers (2)	¾" × ¾" × 93½"	Pine
F Nailers (2)	¾" × ¾" × 43½"	Pine
G Collector panel (1)	½" × 45" × 93½"	Plywood
H Insulation (1)	¾" × 43½" × 92"	Polyiso
I Nailers (3)	¾ × ¾ × 95"	Pine
J Upper nailer (1)	¾" × 1½" × 45"	Pine
K Caps (2)	¾ × ¾" × 48"	Cedar or PT
L Glazing supports ½" (2)	½" × 46½"	EMT
M Glazing (2)	¼" × 2' × 8'	Polycarbonate
N Heat collectors (24)	28" × 6¾"	Aluminum soffit panels
O Heat collectors (8)	4" × 84"	Aluminum coil stock
P Long tube (8)	½ × 85½"	Type L copper
Q Tee (14)	½ to ¾"	Copper fitting
R Elbow (2)	½ to ¾"	Copper fitting
S Connector (14)	¾" × cut to fit	Type L copper
T In/Out Pipe (8)	¾" × cut to fit	Type L copper

How to Make a Copper Tubing Heater Panel

The frame that houses this solar water heater is constructed from 2 × 4 and 2 × 6 dimensional lumber. Cut the pieces of the frame to length, then join them with 2½" deck screws driven into pilot holes.

Cut the ¼" plywood to size, then set it inside the frame as a spacer for the ¾ × ¾" nailers. If you can't locate ¾ × ¾" trim stock for the nailers at your building center, rip-cut ¾"-thick strips from a piece of 1× stock (a tablesaw is best for this, but you can use a circular saw and straightedge cutting guide, too). Screw the nailers to the inner perimeter of the frame with 1⅝" deck screws. Check to make sure the plywood is flush in back as you fasten the nailers.

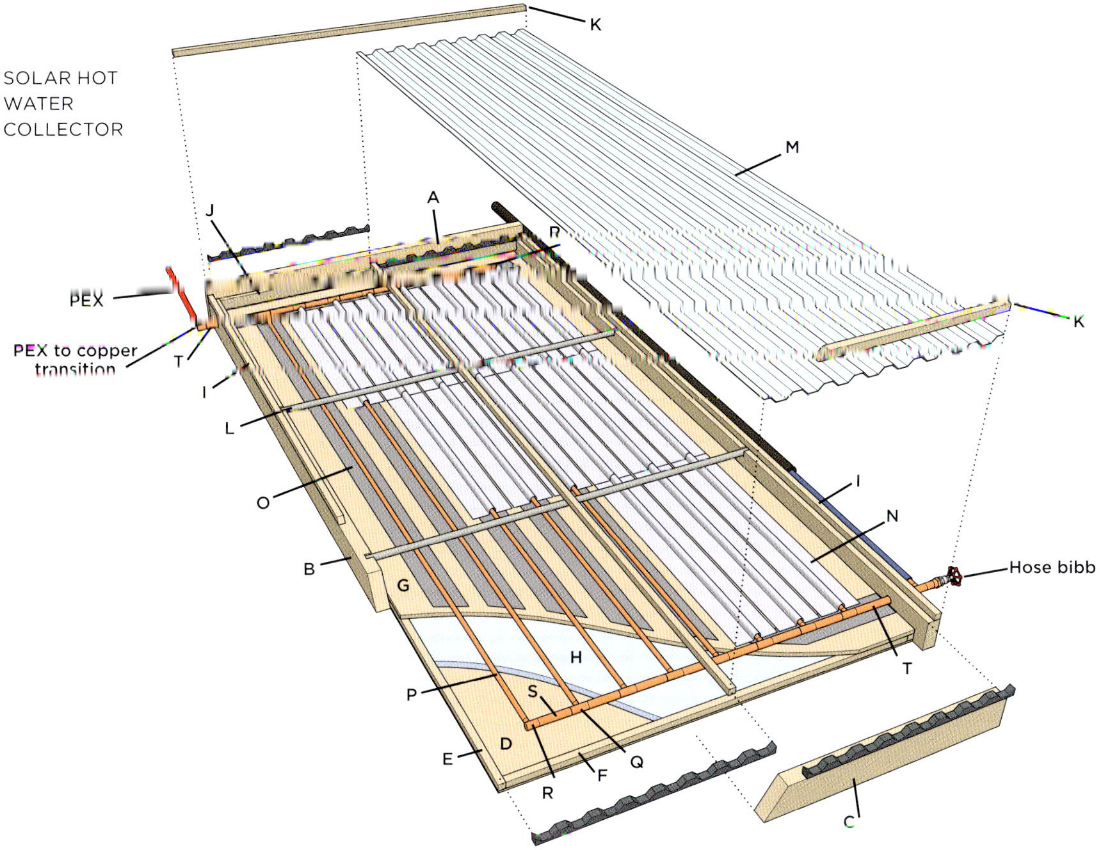

SOLAR HOT
WATER
COLLECTOR

K

M

J

A

PEX

PEX to copper
transition

T

I

L

O

B

G

P

S

H

E

D

F

Q

R

C

I

N

Hose bibb

T

K

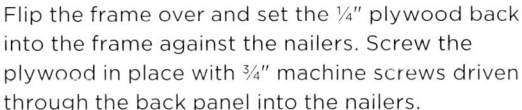

½" Plywood

¾" Insulation

¾" Nailer

3

Flip the frame over and set the ¼" plywood back
into the frame against the nailers. Screw the
plywood in place with ¾" machine screws driven
through the back panel into the nailers.

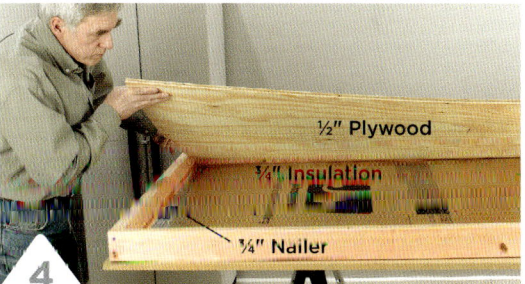

4

Cut panels of ¾"-thick closed-cell, foil-faced
insulation and fit them inside the frame between
the ¾" nailers, flush with the tops of the nailers.
Cut a panel of ½" plywood to fit inside the frame
over the insulation and the nailers and attach
the plywood to the nailers, driving a 1¼" screw
every 10 to 12" around the perimeter. Caulk the
gap between the ½" plywood and the frame with
clear, 100% silicone caulk.

(continued)

5

The "guts" of this solar water heater is an array of copper tubing through which the water runs to absorb heat while it resides inside the box. The matrix of copper tubes is assembled using ¾-to-½ reducing Ts connected by short lengths of ¾" tubing on the ends and long lengths of ½ tubing filling out the space from end-to-end. Making this copper "manifold" requires that you be able to solder copper plumbing pipe. Cut all the copper pieces to length, then clean, flux and assemble them into the grid as seen in the Diagram on page 91. Make the inlet and outlet pipes a few inches longer than you need—they'll be cut shorter after pressure-testing the completed manifold.

6

Solder all the pieces together. Protect the floor from drips of solder and flux with a dropcloth. Wait at least 5 minutes to touch the copper after soldering it—it will be very hot.

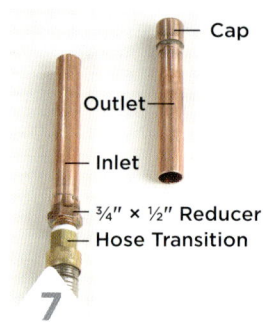

Cap —
Outlet —
Inlet —
¾" × ½" Reducer —
Hose Transition —

7

Before placing the manifold in the collector box, test the manifold for leaks. Solder a cap to the outlet at the top, then solder a ¾ × ½" reducer/ male coupling to the inlet at the bottom. Wrap the threads with teflon tape, then attach the hose transition (available at home centers). Attach a hose and turn the water on. Leave it on for a few minutes; if there's a leak in one of the joints, you'll hear air and then water hissing out. If there are no leaks, drain the water and cut the cap and the reducer coupling off, then shorten both pipes to 5" measured from the last T.

8

Mark the location of the cold-water inlet and the warm-water outlet on the sides of the box by setting the copper grid into the box and extending the inlet and outlet port locations onto the outside of the frame. Drill the holes with a 1"-diameter bit.

9

Mark the manifold locations on the plywood, then cut 4"-wide pieces of aluminum flashing and staple them so they are centered under each length of copper. These will help transfer the heat to the copper pipes. Use stainless-steel staples.

10

There are a few suppliers for preformed aluminum fins (see Resources, p. 136), but you can easily make your own using aluminum soffit panels, a plywood jig and a sledgehammer. Build a jig to make your aluminum fins using two pieces of ⅝"-thick plywood or hardwood screwed to a plywood base. Space the gap between the two plywood pieces by using the ⅝" steel rod and two scraps of aluminum soffit as a guide. Buy solid (not vented) soffit panels with V-grooves and then cut the panels using a razor knife and straight edge into 6¾"-wide strips with the V-groove in the center. The V-grooves are then formed into round channels that fit tightly over the copper pipe. Form them by pounding a ⅝"-dia. steel rod down into them with a sledgehammer (or similar heavy weight).

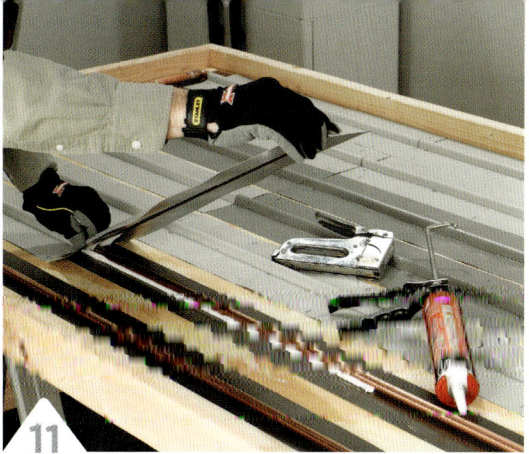

11

Fasten the manifold in place with copper pipe straps, equidistant from the edges. Spread a bead of silicone caulk on both sides of the copper pipe to fill the void along the bottom edge, then push the aluminum fin sections over the pipe and staple or screw them down as close as possible to the pipe. (The silicone helps to transfer heat from the fin to the copper.) Butt the fins against each other.

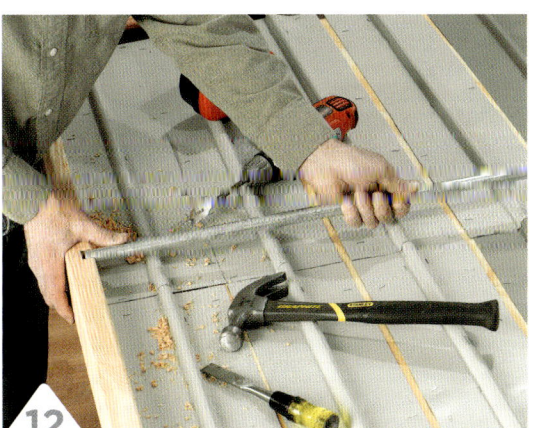

12

Create cross-bar supports for the polycarbonate glazing by installing two lengths of ½" EMT conduit across the box. Drill ¾" holes halfway through the 2 × 4 sides, centering the drill bit ⅜" down and drilling from the inside. Square the holes with a chisel, then place the conduit in the holes.

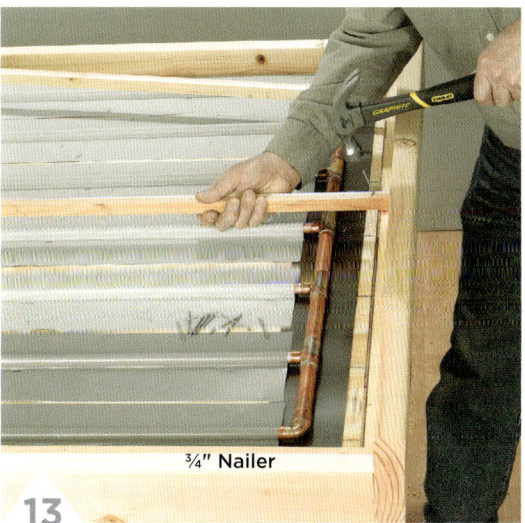

¾" Nailer

13

Lay the glazing on top of the box and mark the spots for ¾" nailers at the sides and the center overlap. Fasten the strips with 6d galv. casing nails.

(continued)

14

Paint the entire inside of the collector with black, high-temperature paint.

Screws with neoprene washers

15

Place closure strips at the top and bottom and lay the corrugated glazing in place. Caulk the overlap between the two panels with a thin bead of clear silicone. Predrill the screw holes on the sides, then enlarge the holes in the glazing with a ¼" bit so that the glazing can move with temperature changes. Fasten the glazing with neoprene screws every foot on the sides. In the center, predrill with a smaller bit and use ½" machine screws every two feet. Squirt a dab of silicone in and around these holes before tightening the screw to seal around the screw.

16

Cover the ends of the glazing with ¾" wood strips. Predrill and fasten the strips with 2½" deck screws. Caulk the strip at the top against the 2 × 6 cap using paintable acrylic caulk.

17

Solder on the last copper fittings and the PEX (crosslinked polyethylene) adapters. PEX is easier to snake through the house than rigid copper. It also makes it possible to adjust the collector angle if you need to, and will flex easily if the collector moves due to soil movement or accidental bumps. Attach it to the brass PEX adapter with a brass ring and a special crimping tool. Finally, seal the inlet and outlet holes with caulk and paint the exterior of the box. Wrap pipe insulation around the exposed copper and PEX lines, both to retain heat and to protect the PEX from UV degradation. Complete the connections inside, then fill the system (see p. 97).

A QUICK GUIDE TO SOLDERING COPPER

There's quite a bit of cutting and soldering involved in this project, and if you've never worked with copper it can seem intimidating, but as long as you follow the correct procedure and use the right tools, you'll be an expert in no time. The most important thing to remember is to test your work after you're done, so you can fix any problems before they cause real damage.

Clean the end of each pipe by sanding with emery cloth. Ends must be free of dirt and grease to ensure that the solder forms a good seal.

Clean the inside of each fitting by scouring with a wire brush or emery cloth.

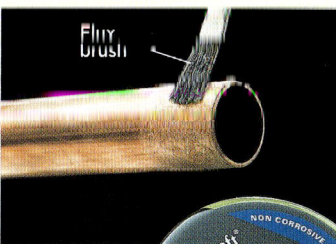

Apply a thin layer of soldering paste (flux) to end of each pipe, using a flux brush. Soldering paste should cover about 1" of pipe end.

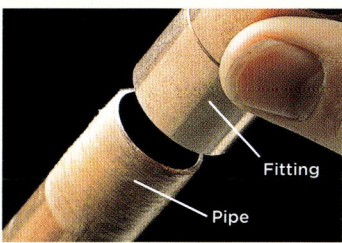

Assemble each joint by inserting the pipe into the fitting so it is tight against the bottom of the fitting sockets. Twist each fitting slightly to spread soldering paste.

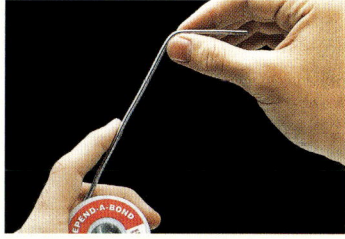

Prepare the wire solder by unwinding 8" to 10" of wire from spool. Bend the first 2" of the wire to a 90° angle.

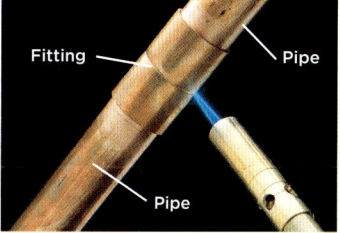

Move the torch flame back and forth and around the pipe and the fitting to heat the area evenly.

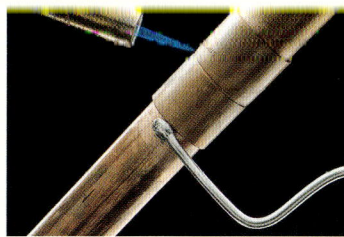

Heat the other side of the copper fitting to ensure that heat is distributed evenly. Touch solder to pipe. Solder will melt when the pipe is at the right temperature.

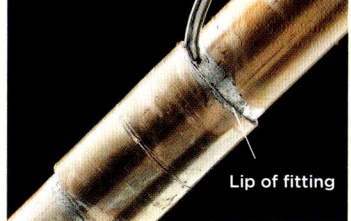

When solder melts, remove the torch and quickly push ½" to ¾" of solder into each joint. Capillary action fills the joint with liquid solder. A correctly soldered joint should show a thin bead of solder around the lips of the fitting.

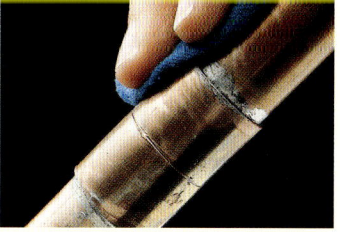

Allow the joint to cool briefly, then wipe away excess solder with a dry rag. Caution: Pipes will be hot. If joints leak after water is turned on, disassemble and resolder.

THERMOSYPHONS

Thermosyphon water heaters are the simplest type of solar water heating system; they don't require pumps or controls to move the hot water and can be used to heat house water directly, without a heat exchanger. However, they do require a storage tank, both to collect and store heated water and to keep it flowing through the collector. If house water were run through the heater without an intermediate storage tank it would either stagnate and get too hot when it wasn't being used, or flow through too quickly to get hot—like a hose lying in the sun.

The syphoning action that circulates the water starts when water in the copper pipes slowly warms up, becomes lighter (hot water weighs less than cold water), and rises through the collecter and then uphill to the top of the storage tank. As the water rises it pulls cool water down from the bottom of the storage tank into the collector. This process continues as long as the water in the storage tank is cooler than the water in the collector. At night the water in the collector is cooler and heavier so it stays in the collector.

When the hot water in the house is turned on, hot water from the storage tank flows into the cold water inlet of the hot water heater, reducing or eliminating the need for electricity or fuel to heat the water. Cold water from the house supply line then flows into the storage tank and from there to the collector.

There are two major tradeoffs for this simplicity: The first is that the system has to be closed off and drained in the winter, unless it's installed in a part of the country where freezing temperatures are rare. The second is that the storage tank has to be at least a foot above the level of the top of the solar collector or the thermosyphon effect won't work. Heated water won't flow downhill and cold water won't flow uphill unless you install a thermostatically controlled water pump between the storage tank and the solar collector.

In warm parts of the world, the storage tank and collector can be set on the roof, as long as the tank is higher. In northern climates it's safer to put the tank inside the house as we did.

Since the thermosyphon collector heats pressurized water from the house water system, the storage tank has to be both insulated and constructed to hold pressurized hot water. Storage tanks with all the necessary inlets and outlets are available through plumbing supply stores and internet suppliers, but the least expensive way to make one is to adapt a new or slightly used electric tank, which already has the inlets and outlets along with a pressure relief valve (always necessary in any pressurized hot water heating system, even a solar-heated one). However, even if you live in the south, this type of tank must be kept inside the house because it doesn't have a weatherproof exterior.

Thermosyphon tanks must be above the level of the collector in order for the movement of water by thermosyphoning to occur.

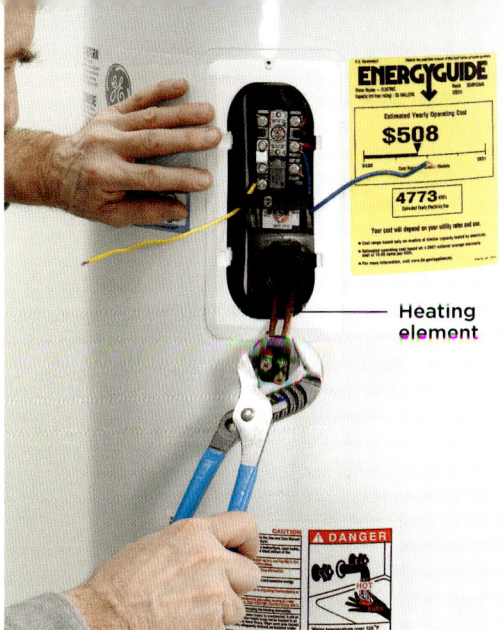

Turn off and disconnect any wiring to the heater you'll be converting to a storage tank. Remove the covers over the heating elements, cut away the wiring, then turn out both heating elements with a socket wrench or a channel lock wrench.

Solder several inches of ¾" pipe to 1 × ¾" reducers so you don't have to use the torch near the plastic and insulation in the water heater. After the pipes cool, wrap the fittings with teflon tape, then thread them into the water heater. Tighten with a wrench, then connect to the PEX lines coming from the solar collector. Connect the house cold water supply to the cold inlet at the top, then connect the hot output to the cold inlet at the main hot water heater.

Cool water flows from the bottom of the storage tank (1) to the solar collector, is heated and becomes lighter, then flows to the upper part of the storage tank (2). Water continues to flow until the water in the storage tank is the same temperature as, or warmer than, the water in the solar collector. When hot water is needed, water from the storage tank flows into the cold water inlet of the water heater (3), then to the fixture (4). Cold water from the main supply then flows into the storage tank to be heated (5). In winter, water to the solar collector is shut off (6), and the system is drained (7 and 8). During the winter cold water continues to flow through the storage tank, where it slowly warms to room temperature, reducing the amount of energy needed to heat it. The storage tank can be closed off from the system (9) if necessary, and water can flow directly to the water heater (10). When the solar collector and tank are being filled, the vent/shutoff at the top of the hot water line from the collecter can be opened to vent air.

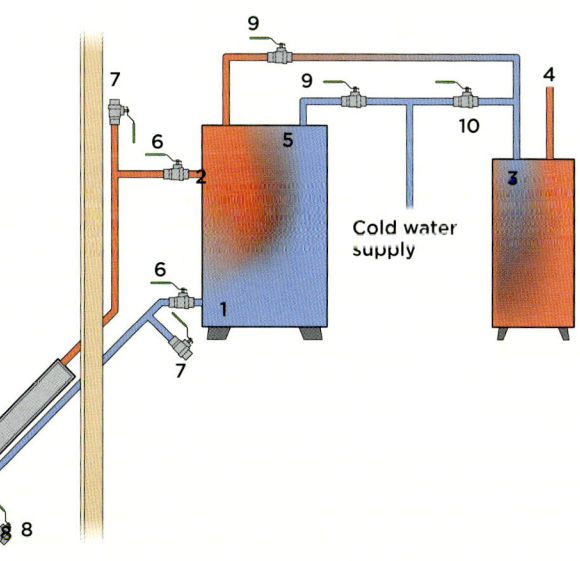

STORAGE TANK FOR A DRAINBACK SYSTEM

Drainback systems are a tried-and-true option for creating your own hot water from solar heat without worrying about the water freezing on cold nights. The same type of solar collector is used as in a thermosyphon system, but the storage tank can be anywhere inside the house, and the water flow is controlled by a pump. The water in the collector is not pressurized or tied into the potable water system. Heat passes to the pressurized house water system through a heat exchanger—in this case a coil of PEX tubing inside a large storage tank. A temperature sensor on the solar collector turns the pump on when the temperature in the collector is hotter than the temperature in the storage tank, and also turns it off if the water is getting too hot. When the pump is off the water drains back into a storage tank (or separate reservoir in some systems) inside the house. Although power is needed to run the pump and the setup is a little more complicated and expensive than the thermosyphon system, drainback systems are safer and provide more energy savings in cooler climates because they can be used year-round. They are basically automatic, and other than occasionally checking for leaks and general system health, you can safely ignore them most of the time, just like a conventional water heater. A drainback system can also be made large enough to help heat pools and hot tubs, or used as part of a home heating system. An ambitious DIYer with an understanding of plumbing and electricity can build a drainback system, but the plumbing is more complicated, so check the links in the Resources on p. 136 for more technical information before you get started. For this project, we are going to focus on building the storage tank.

Storage tanks with built-in heat exchangers are available through plumbing suppliers or the internet, but even a small 40-gallon tank can cost $1,000 or more. If you have space in a utility area that's well-

You can save money on a solar hot water system by making your own storage tank from wood, insulation and an EPDM rubber liner.

ventilated and has a drain and a solid, flat, waterproof floor (like a concrete floor in a basement or insulated garage), you can build your own holding tank from standard building materials. The total cost is a few hundred dollars and you can do it in a day or two. This type of storage tank works well with a drainback system, because it functions as both the reservoir for water from the collectors and as the heat exchanger. A large storage tank storing water from several solar collectors can also be used to provide heat for a hot water heating system. This type of storage tank can't be used for pressurized water, though; the pressurized water is contained in the heat exchanger pipes that run through the storage tank.

The minimum size of the storage tank must be large enough for the heat exchanger piping that you use. For example, one common design uses a 300-ft. coil of 1" PEX tubing for the heat exchanger, and a coil that size needs roughly 36 × 36 × 30" of space. The bigger the heat exchanger coil, the better, since it's also functioning as storage for the solar-heated hot water that comes out of the house faucets. The maximum size and overall shape depends on the space you have available and on the size of your collectors. For a 4 × 8-ft. solar collector, a 36 × 36 × 30" storage tank is more than adequate; it takes longer to heat up than a 40-gallon tank, but that means it will retain the heat longer. Generally, a larger tank is better—it doesn't cost much more to build, and you can always add another collector or reduce the amount of water in the tank.

Use rigid insulation on the inside of the tank, both to cushion the EPDM rubber liner and to eliminate heat loss through the wood. Use polyisocyanurate insulation for at least the first layer of insulation under the EPDM; it has a higher R-value, but it also holds up to high heat better than other types of rigid insulation.

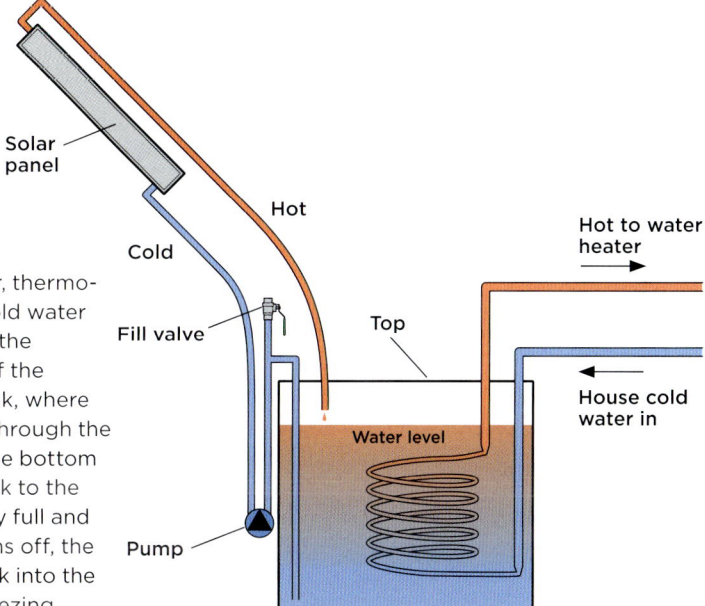

When the sun warms the solar collector, thermostatic controls turn the pump on and cold water is pumped from the storage tank up to the collector. Hot water flows out the top of the collector and down into the storage tank, where the heat is absorbed by water flowing through the heat exchanger coil. Cool water from the bottom of the storage tank is then pumped back to the collector. The storage tank is only partly full and not pressurized, so when the pump turns off, the water in the collector simply drains back into the storage tank, which protects it from freezing.

TOOLS & MATERIALS

For tank size–3 × 3 × 3' inside

Circular saw

Miter saw

Drill/driver with bits

Caulk gun

Razor knife

4' level

Scissors

Stapler

Clamps

2 × 4" × 8'

½" × 4 × 8' sheets plywood

¾" × 4 × 8' sheet plywood

¾ × 6 × 8 plastic composite deckboards

1" × 4 × 8' sheets rigid polyisocyanurate insulation

12 × 16 ft. 45-mil EPDM liner

2" × 4 × 8' XPSpolystyrene insulation

1½" × 4 × 8' XPS polystyrene insulation

1⅝" and 2½" deck screws

Construction adhesive compatible with foamboard

Stainless-steel staples

Silicone caulk

300' roll of 1" PEX tubing

¾" PEX (as needed)

¾" PEX elbows

¾" PEX T

¾" shutoff (for PEX)

(2) 1" × ¾" PEX coupling

Thermostatic controller for pump

Inline or submersible pump (for drainback system)

(2) Strips weatherseal

(continued)

CUTTING LIST

KEY / PART / NUMBER	DIMENSION	MATERIAL
A Frame (8)	1½" × 3½" × 41"	SPF
B Studs (12)	1½" × 3½" × 33½"	SPF
C Frame (8)	1½" × 3½" × 48"	SPF
D Frame (2)	1½" × 3½" × 47"	SPF
E Frame (2)	1½" × 3½" × 44"	SPF
F Base, top (2)	¾" × 48" × 48"	Plywood
G Sides (2)	½" × 41" × 38"	Plywood
H Sides (2)	½" × 40" × 38"	Plywood
I Rail (2)	1" × 5½" × 37"	Composite decking
J Rail (2)	1" × 5½" × 48"	Composite decking
K Insulation (2)	2" × 48" × 48"	Polystyrene
L Insulation (2)	1" × 40" × 40"	Polyisocyanurate
M Top Insulation (1)	1" × 48" × 48"	Polyisocyanurate
N Insulation (2)	1" × 40" × 36"	Polyisocyanurate
O Insulation (4)	1" × 38" × 36"	Polyisocyanurate
P Insulation (2)	1" × 36" × 36"	Polyisocyanurate
Q Outer insulation (4)	1½" × 33½" × 15¼"	Polystyrene
R Outer insulation (4)	1½" × 33½" × 16¾"	Polystyrene
S Strap (8)	1½" × 12"	Galvanized metal strap

STORAGE TANK

The weight of the container with 30" of water inside is roughly 1500 lbs. The capacity is 175 gallons, with 6" of air space.

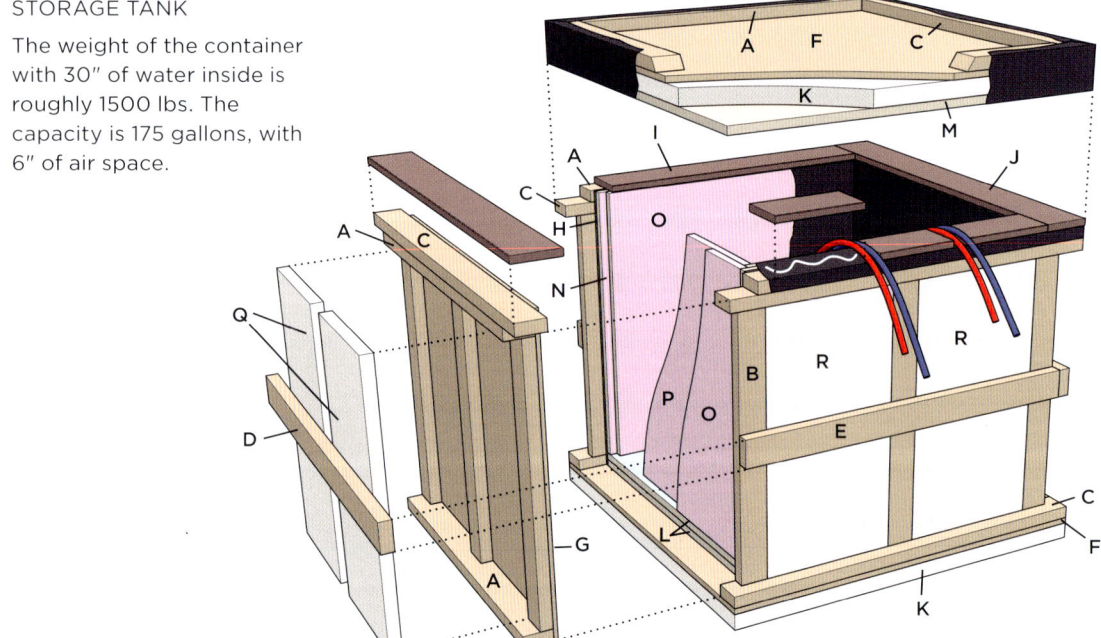

How to Build the Tank

Select a flat, level area of floor for the storage tank, preferably not too far away from the plumbing for your solar collector and water heater. When the tank is full of water it will weigh roughly 1500 lbs, so it needs to sit on a solid, flat base. If the floor is uneven, level it with floor leveler or build a wood platform. Although the tank will be sealed shut with no penetrations through the liner, with this much water it's best to be prudent and place the tank in the vicinity of a floor drain or an area where water won't cause any damage. And be sure to keep the tank bolted shut, especially if you have kids—the water inside can get dangerously hot.

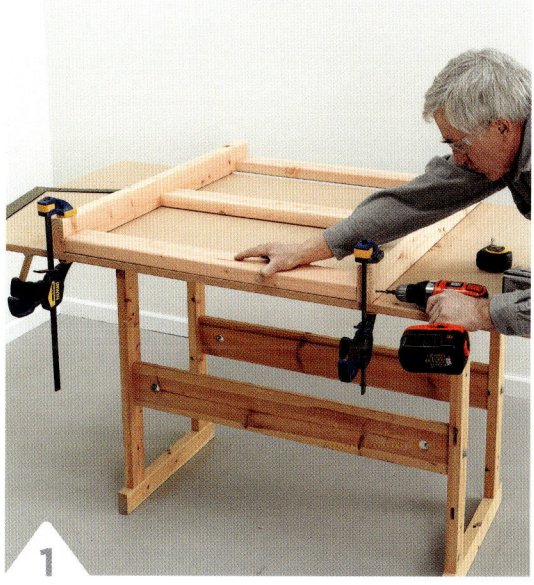

Screw two of the 41" 2 × 4s to three vertical 2 × 4s, then fasten the 11" wide piece of ½" plywood to the 2 × 4s with construction adhesive and 1⅝" screws. Repeat for the opposite side. Align the bottom edge of the plywood with the bottom 2 × 4; the top edge will overhang 1½".

Assemble the remaining sides, but instead of aligning the horizontal studs with the edge, fasten them 2" in from the edges. Place the third stud in the center.

(continued)

3

Place the ¾" plywood base at the tank location, then assemble the short sides to the long sides, fastening the overlapping corner 2 × 4s together with the long deck screws.

4

Turn the box on its side. Fasten the plywood sides in place on the long walls, taking care to align corners and edges. Check the box for square as you assemble it.

Base

5

Tip the box over, then glue and screw the plywood base to the 2 × 4 frame, aligning all the edges.

6

Glue the 2" foam base to the plywood base with construction adhesive, then turn the box right-side up and add the second layer of 2 × 4s to the top, overlapping the corners for strength. Screw the plywood walls to the final layer of 2 × 4s.

7 Place the insulation inside the box, using the foamboard adhesive to attach it. You don't need much; the water will hold the insulation in place. Add the second layer, then seal all the corners on the bottom and sides with silicone caulk.

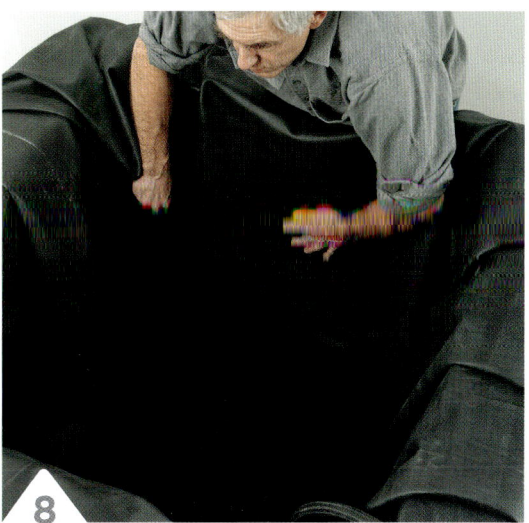

8 Cut and set aside a 5 × 12-ft. piece of the EPDM for the top, then fold the remainder into the tank. Work it into the corners, leaving the rubber loose at the bottom so it doesn't stretch with the weight of the water. Add 6″ of water to hold the rubber in place as you fold over the corners. Drape the excess over the sides.

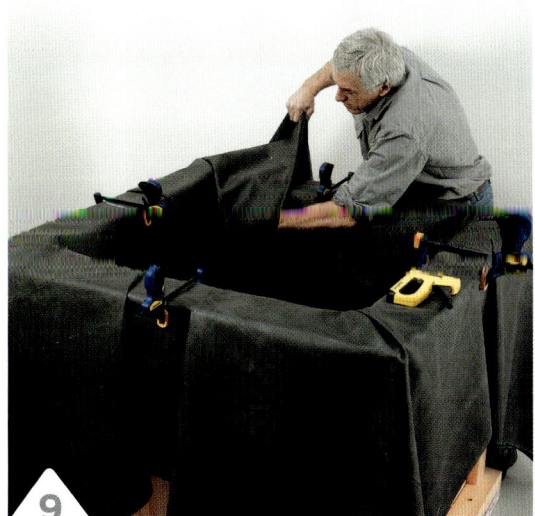

9 Fold the corners as neatly as possible and clamp them in place. Don't stretch the rubber—leave it sagging at the bottom.

10 Staple the rubber around the outside edge of the top 2 × 4 ledge.

(continued)

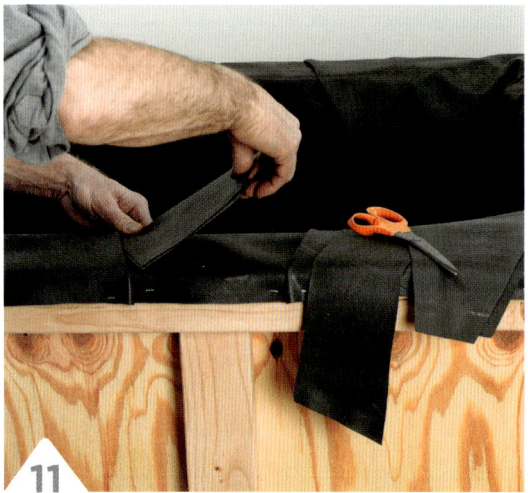

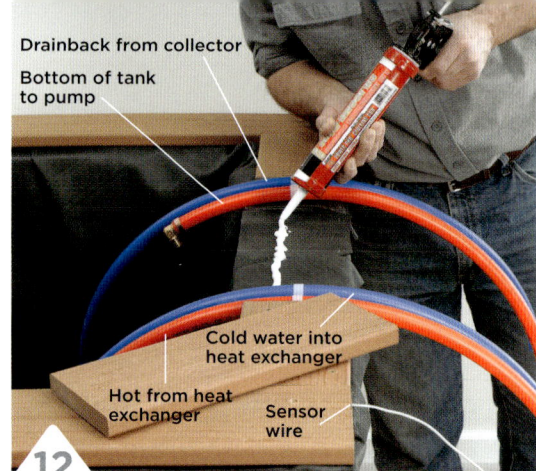

11

Level out the rubber ledge between the corner folds with scrap pieces of rubber.

Decide on a plumbing layout and strap stubs of ¾" PEX to the top edge for the plumbing connections. Purchase a thermostatic controller for the pump that will circulate water between the tank and the solar collector, and run one of the sensor wires into the tank. Cut the pieces of ¾ × 6 cap, then set them on a bead of silicone and screw them in place with 2½" deck or stainless steel screws. *NOTE: if you use copper instead of PEX, complete all soldered connections into and out of the tank before placing the copper to avoid melting the EPDM liner.*

13

Construct the top from 2 × 4s, ¾" plywood, 1½ or 2" rigid foam, and 1" polyiso. Cut a 5-ft. square of rubber liner for the top, with 6" cutouts at each corner. Fold the flaps up the sides and over the top, then staple the rubber in place.

14

Place 1½" pieces of insulation on the sides, then install horizontal 2 × 4s around the center. If desired, you can add additional pieces of insulation above and below the 2 × 4s, then cover the sides with ¼" plywood for a finished appearance.

Set the 1" PEX tubing into the tank, then connect the ends to the incoming and outgoing ¾" tubing with PEX 1 × ¾" reducers. Leave enough slack in the PEX lines so that they can move around as they fill. After making the connections, temporarily hook one end (outside the tank) to the water hose and plug the other end, then turn the water on and check for leaks in your connections. Then fill the tubing with water. *TIP: Wrap a concrete block in EPDM and set it in the bottom to keep the PEX tubing above the cooler water at the bottom.*

Add two strips of weatherseal on the ledge about 2" apart. Use a soft foam type that compresses easily and fills voids, like this.

Complete the plumbing connections inside the tank, fill gaps around the pipes on the ledge with silicone, then clamp the top down tightly to seal the edges. Fasten the top to the base with galvanized strap and deck screws.

Adding Water

The water used in the collecter tank is pumped to the solar collector, heated, and then drained back to the tank, dripping into the air space. It is at atmospheric pressure and is not connected to the house water system. If possible, use distilled water for the tank to avoid mineral deposits. If that's too expensive, house water will work. If all the openings are well-sealed and there are no leaks, the tank will stay full. Drain the old water and replace it every year or two.

Add the water to about six inches from the top after making all the plumbing connections and filling the PEX tubing. Test the system before sealing the top to make sure everything works.

Check the water level from time to time, especially in the first months. You can either just open the top, or else drill a hole for a ½" pipe in the top, seal around it, put a threaded cap on, and then check the water level with a dipstick.

Installing a Tempering Valve

Solar hot water can get dangerously hot on sunny summer days—up to 180°F, much hotter than the 120°F water in a typical hot water heater. To avoid scalding when using solar hot water, add a tempering (or mixing) valve above the hot water outlet on the hot water heater—a valve that automatically lowers the temperature of hot water when necessary by mixing in cold. Installation is straightforward. Turn off the hot and cold water and drain the system, then cut the supply pipes as necessary and install the valve.

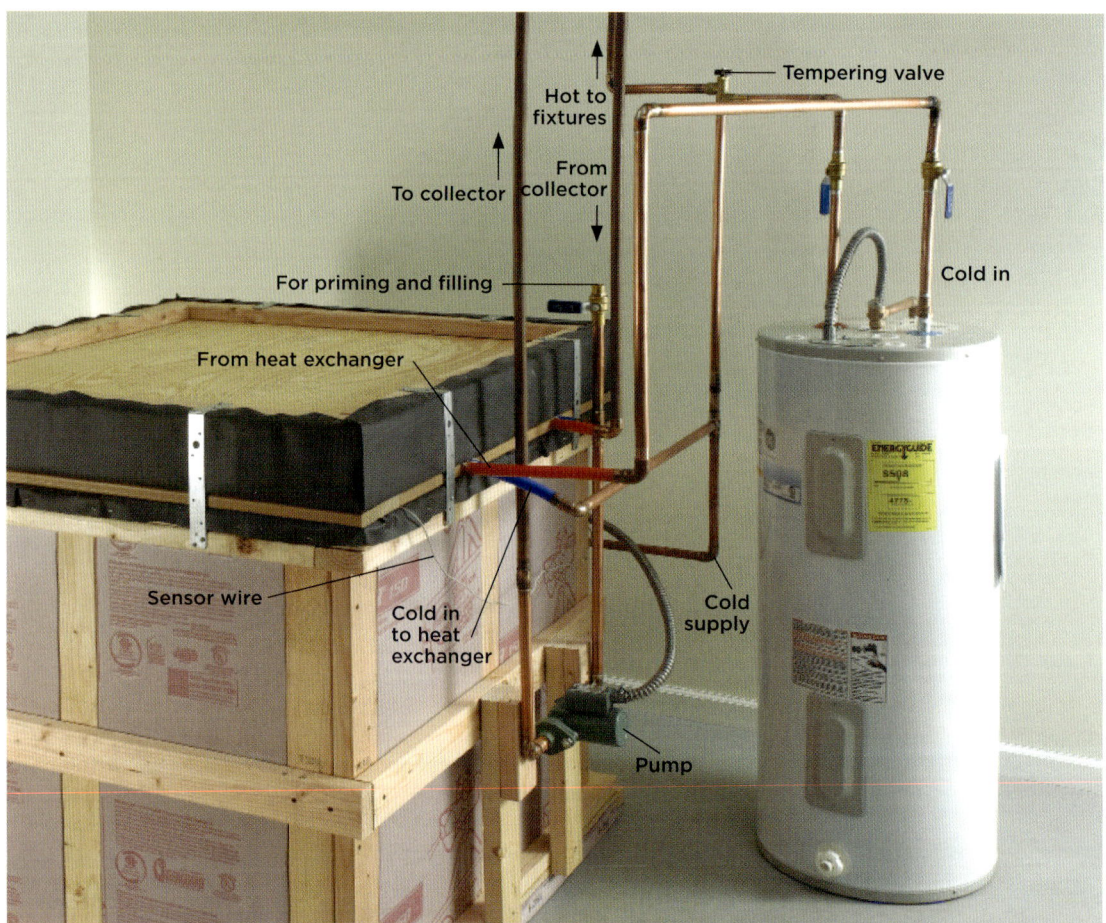

Most external pumps are water-lubricated, and since water seeks its own level the pump should be attached near the bottom of the tank. Connect the pump to the cold-water side of the system, to a pipe run to the bottom of the tank, and prime it with water before turning the system on for the first time. Different solar collector systems need different size pumps: consult the dealer or a professional installer for help selecting the right size. Wire the pump to a power source and to a "differential controller"—a type of thermostatic control that switches on when the collector is warmer than the storage tank, following the instructions for the control. Connect the water lines to the collector and to the potable water lines as shown in the photo. *NOTE: Use pipe straps and blocking as necessary to secure the pipes. We've omitted them from this photo for clarity.*

Install the tempering valve on the hot water line after it comes out of the heater, before it goes to any fixtures. Connect it to the cold water line. Then reconnect the hot water supply for the house fixtures to the outlet marked "Mix." If you buy a valve with sweat connections, remove the knob and the thermostatic control inside the valve before soldering, then reinstall them when the pipes are cool.

OTHER TYPES OF SOLAR COLLECTORS

Pressurized, closed-loop system: This system uses propylene glycol mixed with water, and is commonly used in cold climates. The heat is transferred to a storage tank by way of heat exchanger, and a pump and controller are used to move the antifreeze through the system. In order for the system to be absolutely safe (and to meet code requirements) the heat exchanger pipes must be double-walled, so that if a leak does develop it won't contaminate the potable water. The antifreeze also must be propylene glycol, a less toxic type of antifreeze. Don't use ethylene glycol (the type used in cars).

This type of system requires an expansion tank and other special components, and should be installed only by an expert or by a highly qualified DIYer. Plans and finished work must be approved by a plumbing inspector.

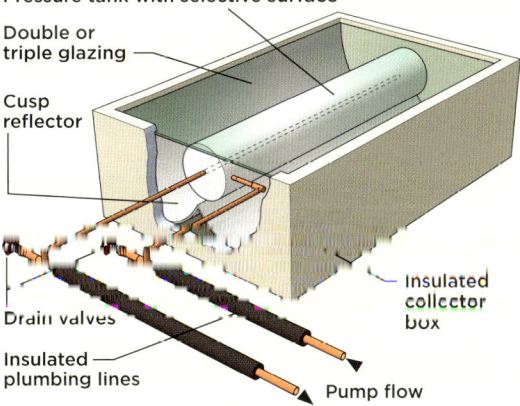

Evacuated-tube collector: *This type of collector has to be purchased from a supplier, although homeowners can install it. Water pipes in this system, instead of running through an insulated box, are installed inside a round tube of insulated glass. The vacuum inside the insulated glass allows light through, but slows heat loss. Evacuated-tube collectors are more efficient than flat-plate collectors in partially sunny or cloudy conditions.*

Batch heaters: *Instead of pipes, the storage tank itself is mounted outside in a large, insulated heat collector box. It can be mounted above or below the water heater, because pressurized house water flows through it whenever hot water is called for. Batch heaters are sold commercially and can also be made from scratch by a resourceful homeowner, but like the thermosyphon system are generally not suitable for cold climates because of the risk of freezing pipe.*

Solar Hot Air Collector—Window Mount

One of the simplest and most cost-effective ways to harvest solar power is with a hot air collector. If you stand in front of a south-facing window on a sunny day, even in winter, you'll understand the basic idea. A solar hot air collector absorbs heat from the sun on a black metal plate in a large, insulated box, then the heat is transferred to cool air flowing over the metal plate from inside the house. As the warmer, lighter air rises out the top of the collector into the house, cooler air from the lower part of the house is drawn in at the bottom of the collector.

Large hot air collectors built into walls are capable of heating a whole house on sunny days. This window collector won't do that unless you live in a super-insulated house, but it can still make a dent in your heating bills. And it's designed to be removable, so in the warm months when you don't need it you can just take out a few screws and store it in the garage, then put the window air conditioner in.

There is no standard size for this collector; make it as wide as your window and 4 to 6 ft. long. The lower end can either be set against the ground, if it's close enough, or attached to the house with wood braces. Place it in a south-facing window that gets at least 5 or 6 hours of direct sun every day, and don't forget to close the flaps when the sun goes down so you don't lose all the heat you gained.

CUTTING LIST

KEY / PART / NO.	DIMENSION	MATERIAL	KEY / PART / NO.	DIMENSION	MATERIAL
A Sides (2)	¾" × 64" × 19"	Plywood	J Upper nailer (2)	¾" × 2½" × 14"	1 × 3
B Ends (2)	¾" × 24⁷⁄₁₆" × 7½"	Plywood	K Top cap (1)	¾" × 10¼" × 25⁷⁄₈"	Plywood
C Stops (2)	1½" × 1½" × 25⁷⁄₈"	2 × 2	L Top door (1)	¾" × 7¼" × 25⁷⁄₈"	1 × 8
D Side nailers (2)	¾" × 2½" × 48"	1 × 3	M Bottom door (1)	¾" × 4" × 25⁷⁄₈"	1 × 6
E End nailer (1)	¾" × 2½" × 20¾"	1 × 3	N Glazing (1)	52" × 25⁷⁄₈"	Polycarbonate
F Back (1)	¼" × 46" × 24½"	Plywood	O Corners (2)	1½" × 1½" × 53"	Aluminum
G Upper back (1)	¼" × 10" × 24½"	Plywood	P Side brace (2)	¾" × 3½" × 25½"	1 × 4 PT
H Divider (1)	¼" × 44" × 22½"	Plywood	Q Back brace (1)	1½" × 3½" × 25⁷⁄₈"	2 × 4 PT
I Upper divider (1)	¼" × 14¼" × 22½"	Plywood	R Heat absorber (1)	44" × 22½"	Aluminum

NOTE: All dimensions are for a 26" wide window opening 4 ft. off the ground. Adjust for your window.

HOT AIR COLLECTOR

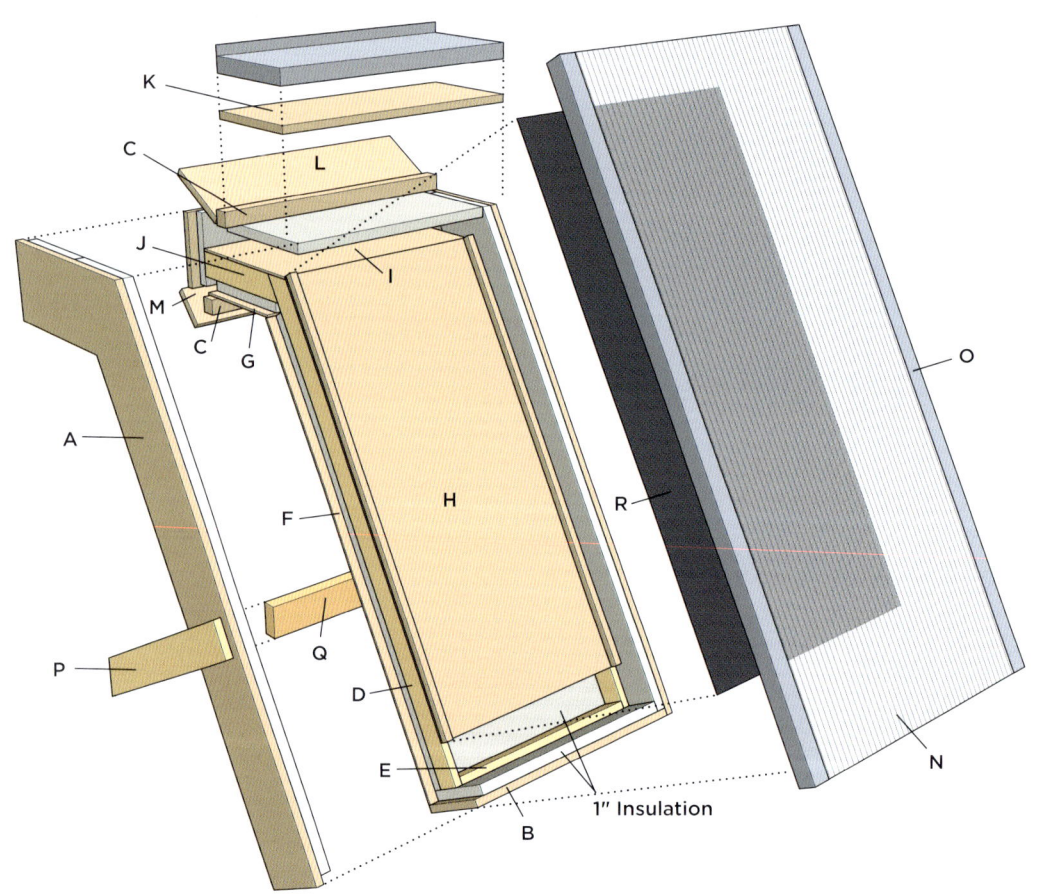

TOOLS & MATERIALS

Circular saw

Miter saw

Jigsaw

Drill/driver with bits

Speed square

Angle measure

4 ft. level

Caulk gun

Razor knife

Tin snips

Clamps

Tape measure

¼" × 4 × 8 plywood

¾" × 4 × 8 AC or BC grade
  (one paint-grade side)
  exterior plywood

1 × 3" × 8' cedar or treated
  (for outside supports)

2 × 2" × width of window pine
  or hardwood

¾ × ¾" × 4'

1" × 8 × 8' (rip to size for doors)

1" × 4 × 8' polylsocyanurate
  insulation

Foam backer rod

Hinges

Self-adhesive weatherseal

Doublewall polycarbonate with
  tape or caps for ends (available
  from glass stores, greenhouse
  suppliers or online)

Black aluminum sheet or 16" wide
  brown aluminum coil stock

Black high heat paint

1½" × 96" × ¹⁄₁₆" thick
  aluminum angle

1" deck screws

1⅝" deck screws

2" drywall screws

1½" neoprene screws

1" metal angle brackets

½" × 6 sheet metal screws
  or stainless-steel staples

Construction adhesive
  (look for quick-gripping
  type compatible with
  foam insulation)

Clear silicone caulk

Aluminum tape

How to Construct the Collector

Mark a piece of plywood at the angle recommended for your latitude—see page 53. This collector will face the sun at a 60° angle, but to make the best use of the plywood we're cutting the short horizontal side, so the speed square is set at 30°. The length of the collector is 4 ft. (measured on the bottom), based on the available space from the window to the ground. The short side is initially cut long, because the easiest way to cut it to exact length is to mark it in place. Make the two sides mirror images, with the best side of the plywood facing out.

Set one of the pieces in the window opening, with the short side level and sitting on the inside sill, and the outside tight against the outside sill. Mark the edge of the inside sill and the inside of the window sash. Mark and cut the end of the short piece 5⅝" from the window sill mark at the bottom. To create a slope and a tight fit with the sash on the top, measure the angle of the bottom of the window sash with an angle measure, then transfer that angle to the top of the plywood, starting at the inside edge of the sash. Trim this top edge with a circular saw.

(continued)

End piece

3 Measure the distance between the stop moldings holding the window sash in, then subtract 1½" to get the length of the end pieces, which fit inside the side pieces. Predrill and screw the end pieces in place, then fasten 2 × 2s across the frame at the sash and sill locations.

4 Line the sides and ends with 1" polyisocyanurate insulation. Leave the foil side facing into the box and glue the insulation in place with construction adhesive. Wrap the exposed upper edges with aluminum foil tape to protect the insulation from UV rays. Cut the insulation ¼" narrower than the plywood sides so that the bottom piece of ¼" plywood will fit in between the sides.

5 Screw the 1 × 3 nailers to the sides of both the long and short pieces using 2¼" screws. Place the nailers 1¼" from the bottom edge to leave room for 1" insulation and ¼" plywood.

6

Fasten ¼" plywood to the top of the 1 × 3 to divide the incoming cool air from the hot air. Leave a 3" gap at the lower end of the plywood for air flow. Butt the two pieces of plywood together at the bend, then cover the small gap with a double layer of aluminum tape. Caulk the gaps at the end and at the corners of the insulation.

7

Turn the box over, then add the 1" insulation to the bottom of the box, then cover it with the ¼" plywood. Glue the plywood to the insulation and screw it to the 1 × 3 nailer with 2¼" screws.

8

Cut two ¾" nailers an inch shorter than the plywood divider, then fasten them to the plywood and the 1 × 3 to create an air channel above and below the heat-absorbing aluminum. Cut the aluminum to fit across the box, then attach it to the nailers with stainless-steel staples or ½" sheet-metal screws. *NOTE: We used a thick, pre-painted aluminum sheet that's available online. If you use aluminum coil stock, paint it black after installing it. See Resources on page 136.*

9

Cut and install 1" insulation to fit the angled top, from the 2 × 2 to the outside corner. Caulk any gaps along the sides. Spread a bead of glue on the insulation, then cover it with ¾" plywood screwed across the top, and extending from the 2 × 2 to 1" beyond the outside corner. Clamp the plywood and insulation until the glue sets.

(continued)

10

Cut the polycarbonate glazing so that it matches the width of the box. Cut it long enough so it tucks under the overhang at the top and hangs over ½" at the bottom. Make sure to install it with the UV-protected side up (the side with the label).

11

The vertical ribs add strength and insulation value to lightweight doublewall polycarbonate, and the two layers help it resist fogging. Cover the top end with waterproof tape and the bottom end with a permeable tape that keeps bugs out.

12

Spread silicone on the plywood edge and set the glazing in place, pushing it under the plywood edge at top and clamping the bottom to hold it in place. Predrill holes in the aluminum corner before you set it in place, and cut the upper end to fit the angle of the top. Spread a bead of silicone about 1" from the outside edge of the glazing and set the aluminum corner over it. Hold the aluminum down firmly and evenly and screw it to the plywood sides with the 1½" screws. Clamp the glazing at the bottom for a few hours until the silicone sets up.

13

Cut aluminum or galvanized coil stock to cover the top, measuring from the 2 × 2. Cut it 3" longer and wider, then clamp the coil stock between the table and a piece of wood and make a 1½" bend at the front and the rear. The front and rear bends should go in opposite directions. Make a 1½" cut on both sides 1½" in from the front and back so that the sides can bend down. Place the coil stock on the top of the plywood, with the back bent up tight against the 2 × 2 so it fits behind the window. Then fold the front down over the glazing and bend the excess back around the sides. Finally, fold the sides down and screw them in place with the ½" screws.

14 Cut 1 x 8s to fit for covers for the inlet and outlet, so that heat won't be lost when the sun goes down. Apply self-adhesive weatherseal around the edges, then screw on two or three hinges, depending on the width of the window. Use hooks to hold the upper cover in place and small barrel bolts to hold the lower cover.

15 Set the solar collector in the window with the inside 2 × 2 tight against the sash and the outside pushed against the sill (you'll need a helper for this). Fasten 1 × 3 supports to the sides, then screw them to the house with metal angle brackets or a 2 × 4 between the supports. Attach the collector to the window sash on the inside with small angle brackets placed on the 2 × 2. Wedge foam backer rod or other type of weatherseal into gaps around the window jamb and into the gap between the upper and lower sash.

WORKING WITH DOUBLEWALL POLYCARBONATE

Doublewall polycarbonate is often used in greenhouses—and for solar projects—because it's lightweight, has some insulation value, and doesn't fog over with condensation. It's also much less expensive, much lighter, and much less breakable than insulated glass. It can be cut easily with a saw, and it transmits almost as much light as insulated glass. Most suppliers carry it in 4 ft. and 6 ft. widths and up to 20 ft. in length (look for greenhouse or plastics suppliers in your area, or check online).

One side of the polycarbonate has UV protection that keeps it from getting hazy and cracked, as happens with standard plexiglas. Make sure you install the panels with this side facing up. Once installed, the top of a panel is sealed with waterproof foil tape or caps; the bottom is sealed with a breathable tape that keeps dust and bugs out but lets moisture drain through.

Polycarbonate is cut and drilled with standard woodworking tools. Use a blade with 10–12 teeth per inch, like a fine-toothed plywood cutting blade. Polycarbonate moves with temperature changes, so drill holes $\frac{1}{16}$" larger than the fasteners and don't overtighten. The panels are fastened with neoprene screws (screws with wide heads and neoprene rubber washers attached). A wide variety of glazing accessories for joints, corners and roof caps is available if you make a larger project.

Hot Air Collector—Roof Mount

The solar hotbox works on the same general principle as the window hot air collector in the previous project, but it's a big step up in size and amount of heat generated. Designed to work with an existing forced-air heating system, this hotbox can carry a substantial amount of the heating load for an average residence—up to 40% for the home where this project was done. With gas prices rising all the time, that can quickly add up to serious money.

As always, the most cost-effective way to save money on energy costs is by sealing air leaks and adding more insulation, but once you've done that, this project is a good next step. Mounted on a south-facing wall or on the roof, the collector takes air from inside your home and blows it through the thermal solar panels, which are essentially a series of metal ducts in a black box under tempered glass. As the air moves through the ductwork, the sun's rays cause it to heat to high temperatures. Then, at the end of the duct, another vent moves the air back into your home's heating ductwork or an interior vent, sending the now-heated air right into the home. It's basically a forced-air heater that uses the sun for heat instead of gas burners.

The flow of air is controlled by a fan and vent dampers. The fan only turns on when the thermostat calls for heat and the temperature in the hotbox is higher than the temperature in the house, so there's no heat loss during the night or on cloudy days, even though the hotbox requires two holes cut in the roof. It's also possible to put a variation of this design on a south-facing wall, as long as it gets at least 6 hours of sunlight per day.

You can build solar hot air panels yourself. The style shown here is simple: essentially, a box, a series of ducts, and a piece of glass. The panels are permanently installed and ducted in to your home, complete with automated thermostatic controls. In this project, we'll walk you through one version of a solar hot air panel designed and installed by Applied Energy Innovations of Minneapolis, Minnesota (see Resources p. 136), with the help of homeowner Scott Travis.

When combined, these three DIY "hotboxes" introduce enough hot air into this home to carry 30 to 40% of the home heating load.

Anatomy of a Hot Air Solar Panel

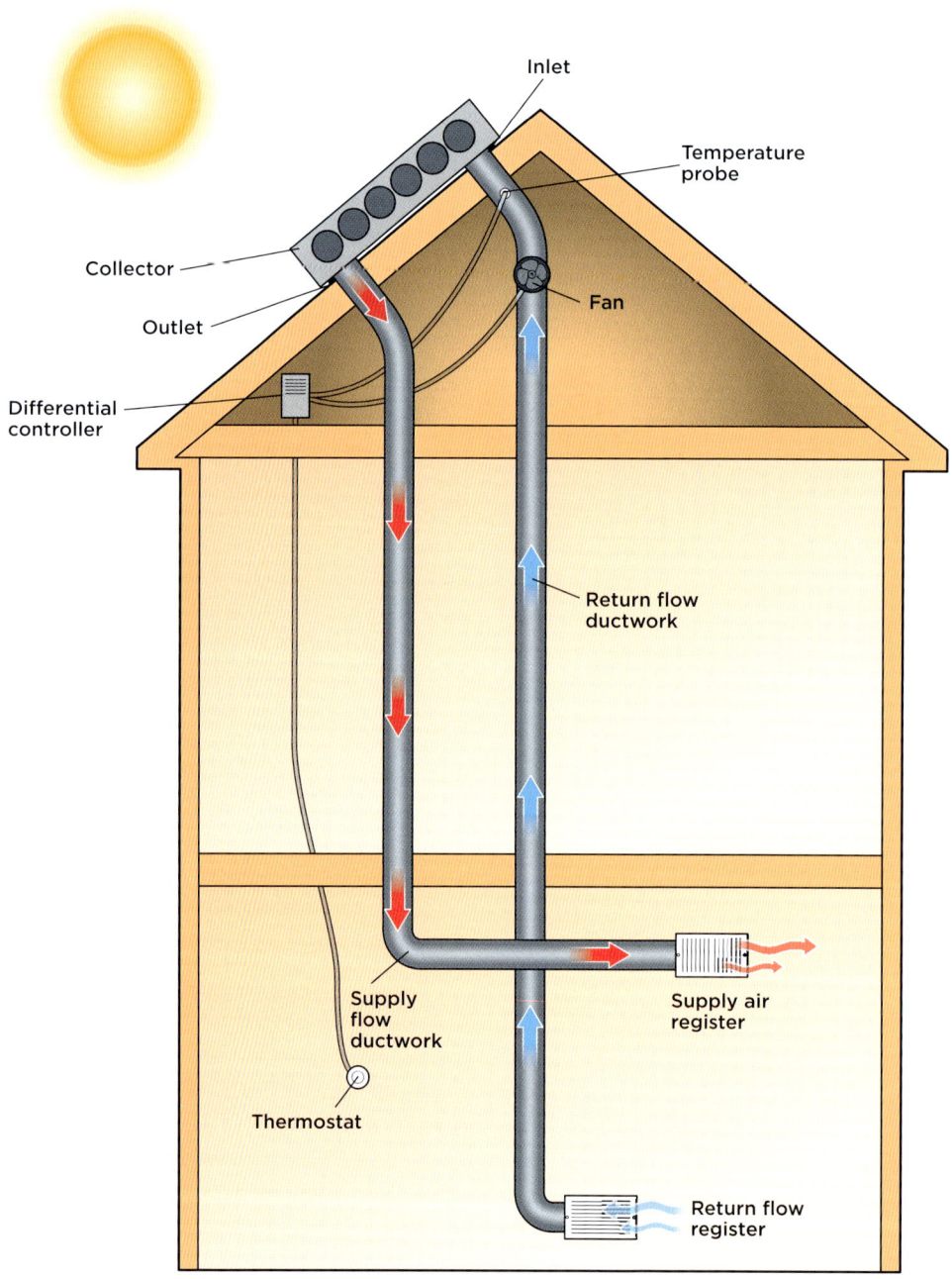

The solar hot box is a very simple system. Cold air from the house is drawn up into a network of ducts in the collector, where it is warmed by the sun then circulated inside to heat the house.

TOOLS & MATERIALS

Metal-cutting saw

Drywall saw

Straightedge

Aviation snips

Tape measure

Temperature controls

Eye and ear protection

Carpenter's square

Drill/driver with bits

⅛" pop rivets

Pop rivet gun

Caulk gun

Aluminum foil tape

Rubber gasket roofing nails

2 × 6 steel studs

Utility knife

8" blower fan

4" hole saw

Trim paint roller

Sheet-metal screws with rubber gaskets

Chalkline

Scissors

Reciprocating saw

Roof jack

High-temperature black paint (matte)

4" aluminum HVAC duct

1"-wide closed-cell foam gasket

4" male and female duct connectors

(2) 8" plenum box

High-temperature silicone caulk

Cardboard

Sheet-metal start collars

Roofing cement

1"-thick R7 rigid insulation

¼" tempered glass

Flashing

Shingles (if needed)

Unistrut

Unistrut connectors

(2) Duct collars

⅜" threaded rod

Spring-fed 8" backdraft dampers

The temperature control equipment opens and closes the damper and causes the blower fan to turn on and off as needed.

(continued)

1 Cut and bend the box frame pieces from 2 × 6 steel studs. Each steel stud piece will wrap two sides of the panel with a 90° corner bend. Mark the bend location on both steel studs. Cut a relief into the 6″ side of the stud with aviation snips at this mark. Bend the stud to an L-shape and use a square to ensure that the corner forms a true 90° angle.

2 Drill ⅛″-dia. holes in the overlapping top and bottom flanges. Clamp the corners together before drilling, using a square to make sure the corner forms a 90° angle.

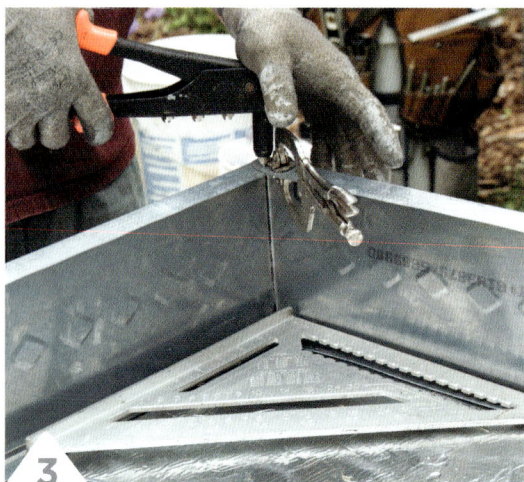

3 Fasten the corners of the metal box with two ⅛″-dia. sheet-metal pop rivets in the top and bottom. Leave one corner open to create access for the insulation panel insert.

4 Cut the foil-faced rigid foam insulation to match the interior dimensions of the box, using a drywall saw or a utility knife.

5 Apply high-temperature silicone to the bottom flanges of the box (inset). Fit the 1" foil-faced from step #4 into the back of the frame, then close up the box and secure the open corner. Cut 5"-wide strips of foam insulation to the length and width of the panel. Place a thick bead of silicone around the outside perimeter of the unit. Insert the strips into the silicone and press tightly against the sides of the panel to hold the backing firmly in place. The foil should be facing into the box.

6 Seal the insulation edges. Place a bead of silicone around the inside corner where the insulation strips and backing panel meet, and then seal with foil tape. Flip the panel over. Place a bead of silicone on the intersection of the 2 × 6 stud flange and the back of the insulation, and seal with foil tape. Conceal any exposed insulation edges with foil tape.

7 Create inlet and outlet holes in the walls with a hole saw or circle cutter. The number and location of the ductwork holes depends on where each panel fits into the overall array (presuming you are making and installing multiple panels). The first and last panels in the series will each have one end wall that is uncut, while intermediate panels will have duct holes on each end wall (inset).

8 Install a compartment separator in the first and last panels with a piece of foil insulation set on edge. Cut ductwork access holes in the separator. Then, cut out holes for the ductwork that will pass through the separator. Also cut a plenum opening in the separated compartment in the first and last unit.

(continued)

9

Paint the entire box interior using black high-temperature paint and allow it to dry completely. A trim roller works well for this task.

10

Insert the ductwork. Beginning at the inlet duct, guide 4" aluminum HVAC ductwork in a serpentine shape throughout the entire multi-panel installation, ending at the outlet duct. Join ends of adjoining duct sections with flexible duct connectors fashioned into a U shape and secured with metal screws and foil tape (inset). Paint each section of ductwork with black high-temperature paint once it is in place.

11

Paint the last section of ductwork and touch up around the interior of the box so all exposed surfaces are black.

12

Affix the glass top. First, double-check that all openings in the panel are adequately sealed and insulated. Then, line the tops of the steel stud frame with foam closed-cell gasket tape. Carefully position the glass on top of the gasket tape, lined up ½" from the outside of the frame on all sides. Then, position foam closed-cell gasket tape around the perimeter of the top of the glass panel.

13

Attach the casing. Work with a local metal shop to bend metal flashing that will wrap your panel box. Attach it around the perimeter of the panel with sheet-metal screws with rubber washer heads. *TIP: Be careful when working around the plenum ductwork. If you set the unit down on its back side, you will force the plenum up and break the seal around the opening.*

14

Mark off the panel layout locations on the roof. Transfer the locations of the 8"-dia. inlet and outlet holes to the roof as well. The location of these holes should not interfere with the structural framing members of your roof (either rafters or trusses). Adjust the panel layout slightly to accommodate the best locations of the inlet and outlet, according to your roof's setup. Cut out the inlet and outlet holes with a reciprocating saw.

15

Use a roof jack or Cone-jack to form an 8"-dia. opening. Apply a heavy double bead of roofing cement along the top and sides of the roof jack. Nail the perimeter of the flange using rubber gasket nails. Cut and install shingles with roofing cement to fit over the flashing so they lie flat against the flange.

16

Attach Unistrut mounting U-channel bars to the roof for each panel. Use the chalklines on the roof to determine the position of the Unistrut, and attach to the roof trusses with Unistrut connectors.

(continued)

17

Hoist the panels into position. Carefully follow safety regulations and use scaffolding, ladders, ropes, and lots of helpers to hoist the panels onto the roof. Wear fall-arresting gear and take care not to allow the plenum ductwork to be damaged.

18

Connect the inlet and outlet ducts on the panel(s) to the openings on the roof. Position the panels so the inlet and outlet openings match perfectly, and attach with a duct collar and silicone caulk.

19

Connect the panels to the Unistrut with ⅜" threaded rod attached at the top and bottom of the panel on the outside. Cut threaded rod to size, then attach to the Unistrut with Unistrut nuts. Attach the top clip to the top of the rod and the front face of the panel. Tighten the assembly to compress the panel down to the Unistrut for a tight hold.

20

Seal the panel connections with 1" foam gasket tape around each end of the panels where they connect. Place a bead of silicone caulk on top of the gasket tape and then attach 3"-wide flashing over the two panels at the joint. Attach flashing to the panel with galvanized sheet-metal screws with rubber gasket heads.

Hook up the interior ductwork, including dampers and a blower fan. The manner in which this is done will vary tremendously depending on your house structure and how you plan to integrate the supplementary heat. You will definitely want to work with a professional HVAC contractor (preferably one with solar experience) for this part of the job.

ANOTHER TYPE OF SOLAR HEATER

Manufactured solar air heaters are available in a variety of sizes and styles and can be built in or attached to an existing wall or roof. Here, a solar air heater was built into the framing of the wall with the siding trimmed around it (see Resources, p. 136).

Solar Still

Make your own distilled water from stream or lake water, salt water, or even brackish, dirty water, using this simple solar distiller. With just a few basic building materials, a sheet of glass and some sunshine, you can purify your own water at no cost and with minimal effort.

Distilled water is not just for drinking, and it's always worth keeping a few gallons of it on hand. Clean water free of chemicals and minerals has a number of valuable uses:

- Always refill the lead-acid batteries used for solar energy systems or automobiles with distilled water
- Water delicate plants like orchids with distilled water; minerals and additives like fluoride or chlorine that are present in most tap water can harm plants
- Distilled water mixed with antifreeze is recommended for car radiators, as it's less corrosive
- Steam irons become clogged with mineral deposits unless you use distilled water

The principle of using the sun's heat to separate water from dissolved minerals has been understood for millenia, salt ponds being the best example of how this knowledge has been put to use in the past. In salt ponds, seawater is drained into shallow ponds and then baked and purified in the sun until all that remains are crystals of salt. In this case, the pure water that gradually evaporated away was considered a useless byproduct, but as far back as the time of the ancient Greeks it was known that seawater could be made fresh and drinkable by this process.

A solar still works like a salt evaporation pond, except that the water that invisibly evaporates is extracted from the air, the minerals and other impurities are left behind and discarded. As the hot, moisture-laden air rises up to the slanting sheet of relatively cool glass sealed to the box, water condenses out in the form of small droplets that cling to the glass. As these droplets get heavier, they roll down the glass to the collector tube at the bottom and then out to the jug.

Distill your own crystal clear, chemical-free drinking water with a solar distiller.

Studies in Distilled Water

The power of the sun is used to remove the water from these shallow evaporation ponds so that valuable salt can be extracted. A solar still uses the same process, but instead captures the purified water.

A glass of icy-cold water shows how a solar still is able to capture pure water. Since the glass panel is cooler than the air inside the still, moisture condenses on it just like it does on this glass. Here the process is slow, but with the heat of the sun driving it a solar distiller works much more quickly.

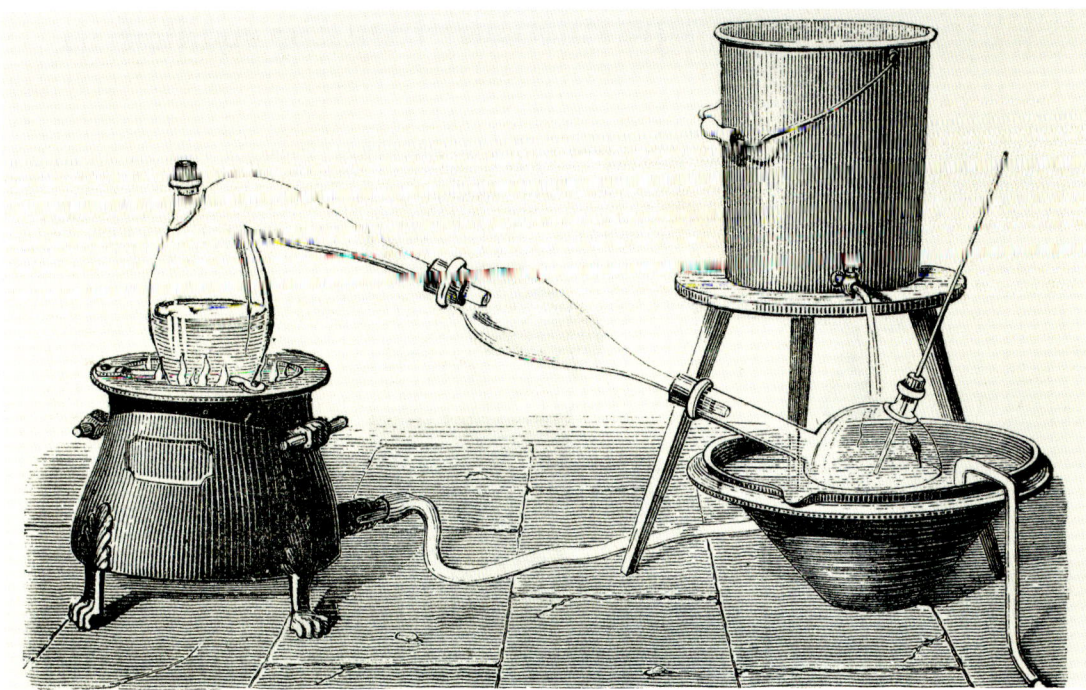

This illustration from a 19th century magazine shows the workings of a distillation apparatus. A gas line feeds a flame that boils a sealed container of water. The steam expands into the glass tube and condenses in another glass vessel immersed in a bowl of cool water. Cool water from the bucket drips steadily into the bowl, keeping the temperature of the water down. The solar distiller works on a similar principle, except the sun is used as a heat source.

This industrial scale desalination plant removes salt and minerals from millions of gallons of water every day.

SOLAR STILL

The box is built from ¾" BC-grade plywood, painted black on the inside to absorb heat. We used a double layer of plywood on the sides to resist warping and to help insulate the box, with an insulated door at the back and a sheet of glass on top.

Finding a good lining or container to hold the water in the inside of the box as it heats and evaporates can be complicated. The combination of high heat and water containing salt or other contaminents can corrode metals faster than usual and cause plastic containers to break down or off-gas, imparting an unpleasant taste to the distilled water. The best liners are glass or stainless steel, although you can also coat the inside of the box with two or three coats of black silicone caulk (look for an F.D.A.-listed type approved for use around food). Spread the caulk around the bottom and sides with a taping knife. After it dries and cures thoroughly, just pour water in—the silicone is impervious to the heat and water.

We chose to paint the inside black and use two large glass baking pans to hold the water. Glass baking pans are a safe, inexpensive container for dirty or salty water, and they can easily be removed for cleaning. We used two 10 × 15" pans, which hold up to 8 quarts of water when full. To increase the capacity of the still, just increase the size of the wooden box and add more pans.

The operation of the distiller is simple. As the temperature inside the box rises, water in the pans heats up and evaporates, rising up to the angled glass, where it slowly runs down to the collector tube and then out to a container.

Turn undrinkable water into pure, crystal-clear distilled water with a home-built solar still.

The runoff tube is made from 1" PEX tubing. Stainless steel can also be used. However, use caution with other materials—if in doubt, boil a piece of the material in tap water for 10 minutes, then taste the water after it cools to see if it added any flavor. If it did, don't use it.

CUTTING LIST

KEY	MATERIAL / NUMBER	DIMENSION
A	Rigid insulation (1)	¾" × 23¾" × 19"
B	Plywood (1)	¾" × 23¾" × 19"
C	Plywood (1)	¾" × 5¾" (high side) × 19"
D	Plywood (1)	¾" × 5⅝" (high side) × 20½"
E	2 × 4 (2)	1½" × 3½" × 22½"
F	Plywood (1)	¾" × 3" × 20½" (long to short edge)
G	Plywood (1)	¾" × 5⅞" × 20½"
H	Plywood (1)	¾" × 9" × 20½" (to long edge)
I	Plywood (2)	¾" × 9⅛" × 5⅛" × 26¾"
J	Plywood (2)	¾" × 8⅞" × 5⅝" × 24½"
K	Tempered glass (1)	27¼" × 22" × ⅛"
L	PEX tubing, cut to length (1)	1"

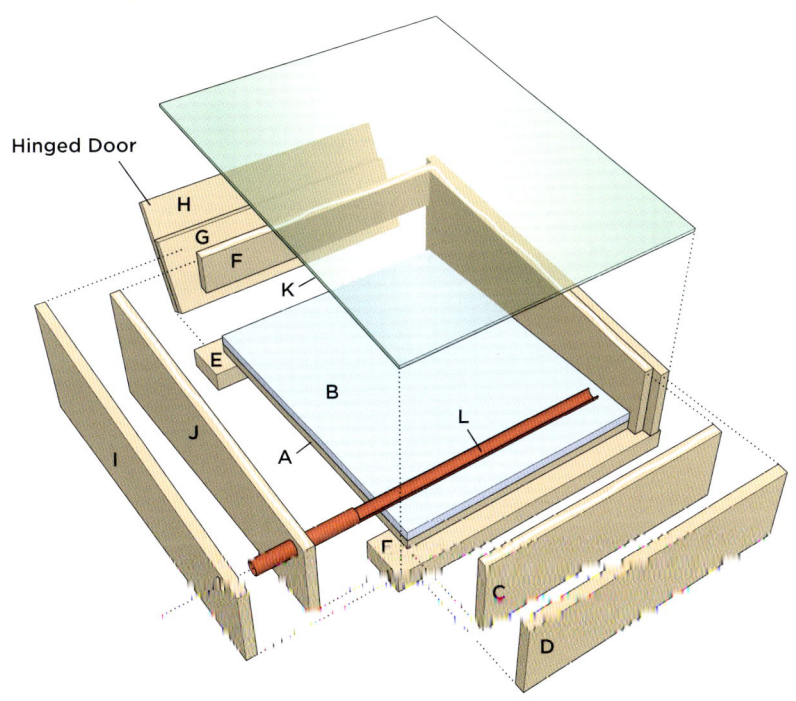

Hinged Door

TOOLS & MATERIALS

Drill/driver with bits	Tape measure	Silicone caulk
Circular saw	2 × 4 × 8' pressure treated	High-temperature black paint
Speed square	(1) ¾ × 4' × 8' sheet of BC exterior plywood	1" PEX tubing
Straightedge	(2) 1½" galvanized hinges	(2) 10" × 15" glass baking pans
Caulk gun	Self-adhesive weatherseal (8')	Wood glue
Razor knife	Knob or drawer pull	1¼", 2", 2½" deck screws
Clamps	27¼" × 22" × ⅛" (minimum) glass	Painter's tape

(continued)

1 Mark and cut the plywood pieces according to the cutting list, p. 131. Cut the angled end pieces with a circular saw or tablesaw set to a 9° angle.

1½"

1¾"

2 Cut the insulation the same size as the plywood base, then screw both to the 2 x 4 supports with 2½" screws.

3 Screw the first layer of front and side pieces to the base and to each other, then add the back piece. Predrill the screws with a countersink bit.

4 Glue and screw the remaining front and side pieces on, using clamps to hold them together as you predrill and screw. Use 1¼" screws to laminate the pieces together and 2" screws to join the corners.

5 Glue and screw the hinged door pieces together, aligning the bottom and side edges, then set the door in position and screw on the hinges. Add a pull or knob at the center.

Foil

6 Paint the inside of the box with black high-temperature paint. Cover the back and the door with reflective foil glued with contact cement. Let the paint dry for several days so that all the solvents evaporate off.

(continued)

7 Apply weatherseal around the edges of the hinged door to make the door airtight.

8 Drill a hole for the PEX drain. The top of the PEX is ½" down from the top edge. Clamp a scrap piece to the inside so the drill bit doesn't splinter the wood when it goes through.

9 Mark the first 19" of PEX, then cut it in half with a utility knife. Score it lightly at first to establish the cut lines.

10 Drill three ⅛" holes in the side of the PEX for screws, then insert the PEX through the hole. Butt it tight against the other side, then screw it in place, sloping it about ¼".

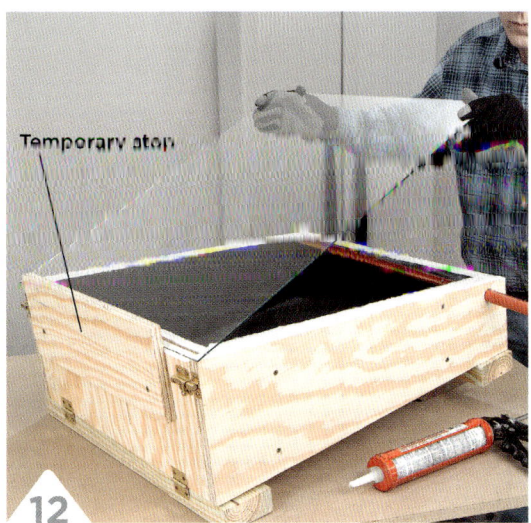

Temporary stop

11 Wipe a thick bead of silicone caulk along the top edge of the PEX to seal it against the plywood.

12 Shim the box level and tack a temporary stop to the top edge to make it easy to place the glass without smearing the caulk. Spread a generous bead of caulk on all the edges, then lay the glass in place. Tape it down around the edges with painter's tape, then let it set up overnight.

Resource Guide

Guide to Federal, State And Local Incentives
DSIRE - Database of State Incentives
for Renewables and Efficiency
www.dsireusa.org

General Information about Solar Energy
Build It Solar
www.builditsolar.com

U.S. Dept. of Energy
www.energy.gov

Florida Solar Energy Center
www.fsec.ucf.edu/en

Home Power Magazine archive
www.homepower.com/home

Find My Shadow (solar position charts)
www.findmyshadow.com

Solar Energy Products and Materials
Real Goods
(866) 596-6940
www.realgoods.com

Backwoods Solar
(208) 263-4290
www.backwoodssolar.com

Northern Arizona Solar and Electric
(800) 383-0195
www.solar-electric.com

Silicon Solar
(800) 786-0329
www.siliconsolar.com

Mounting Systems
IronRidge
www.ironridge.com

Unistrut
https://unistrutohio.com

Unirac
www.unirac.com

Solar Cooking
Solar Cookers International
www.solarcookers.org

Solar Cooker-at-Cantinawest
www.solarcooker-at-cantinawest.com

Solar Oven Society
www.solarovens.org

Solar Hot Water
U.P. Solar Solutions
(888) 744-8797
www.aluminum-solar-absorbers.com

Solar Reflective Foils
Clear Dome Solar Thermal
(619) 990-7977
www.cleardomesolar.com

Solar Air Heaters
Your Home Solar
(865) 226-3101
www.yourhomesolar.com

Polycarbonate Panels
Tuftex
(800) 777-7663
www.tuftexpanel.com

Greenhouse Megastore
(888) 281-9337
www.greenhousemegastore.com

Advance Greenhouses
(877) 238-8357
www.advancegreenhouses.com

Photo Credits

Shutterstock.com: pages 8 (top left and middle), 10, 12, 21 (top left), 21 (bottom left), 23, 24, 25, 28 (top), 29, 31 (bottom right), 32, 33, 35 (bottom), 76, 77, 70, 30, 40, 42, 43, 44, 45 (top), 64, 67 (top left), 68, 69, 73, 77 top, 84, 86, 87, 96, 107 120, 128, 129

iStockphoto.com: pages 27, 31 (top right), 34, 35 (top), 45 (bottom), 66, 67 (top left), 72 (bottom), 77 (bottom)

Active Ventilation Products, roofvents.com: page 31 (bottom left)

US Air Force/Nadine Y. Barclay: page 8 (top right)

Glossary

Absorber Material that captures solar rays (photons) so they may be converted to electrical current (electrons).

Activated shelf life Amount of time a stored battery will hold usable charge.

Alternating Current (AC) Electrical current that is distributed in reversing cycles (60 cycles per second in the U.S.) through wall outlets or a DC to AC converter.

Amorphous silicon A thin film of silicon-base, photovoltaic cells with no crystalline structure, usually applied to a substrate.

Amperage Interrupt Capability (AIC) A rating indicating the highest amount of current a DC fuse will interrupt.

Ampere (amp) A unit of electrical current equal to one volt across one ohm of resistance.

Anode The positive electrode in a battery.

Antireflection coating A thin layer applied to a solar cell surface to limit light loss due to reflection.

Base load The minimum amount of electric power a utility must supply at all times (on average).

Battery Electrochemical cells within a container and connected to provide a proscribed amount of required voltage and current when fully charged.

Battery cycle life The number of charge/discharge cycles a battery can undergo before failing to meet performance specifications.

Btu (British Thermal Unit) A unit for measuring heat output. It is the amount of heat (252 calories) needed to raise the temperature of one pound of water 1°F.

Catastrophe fuse A fuse in a photovoltaic system that is designed to trip and shutoff inflow of current in the event of an extreme power surge, protecting the downstream devices.

Cell One unit of a device that produces direct voltage by converting chemical energy into electrical energy.

Charge controller A device in a photovoltaic system that controls and limits the flow of current from the source and into and out of the battery.

Cloud enhancement The increase in solar intensity caused by light that is reflected by clouds.

Conductor Any material through which electricity is transmitted: usually refers to an electrical wire.

Converter A device that converts electrical current from DC to AC, or vice versa.

Crystalline silicon A photovoltaic cell created with a slice of single-crystal silicon or polycrystalline silicon.

Cutoff Voltage The amount of electrical voltage that, usually in a power surge, causes the charge controller to disconnect the battery from the photovoltaic system.

Deep-cycle battery A type of battery (such as a marine battery) that can endure a high number of charge/discharge cycles.

Diffuse Radiation Solar radiation that has been reflected or scattered by the atmosphere and ground.

Diode An electronic device that restricts current flow to a single direction.

Direct beam radiation Radiation received from direct sunlight.

Direct current (DC) Electrical current that flows in one direction only, usually from a battery and in relatively low voltage (compared to AC).

Discharge The outflow of electrical energy stored in a battery.

Discharge rate The rate at which current flows out of a battery, usually expressed in amperes or time.

Dry Cell A battery that can't be recharged because it has a sealed electrolyte.

Electric circuit A defined path through which electrical current flows out and returns.

Electric current Electrical energy, measured in amperes, that flows through a conductor.

Electrode A conductor that contacts a ground.

Electrolyte A nonmetallic conductor that carries current generated by the movement of ions instead of electrons.

Float charge The amount of voltage required to counteract the natural discharge of a battery so it remains fully charged.

Frequency The number of repetitions, expressed in Hertz (Hz), that a wave repeats to complete a waveform.

Fresnel lens A device formed by concentric rings of lenses that focus light to increase its intensity.

Full Sun The amount of solar power hitting the Earth's surface at noon on a clear day (approximate amount is 1,000 watts per square meter).

Gigawatt (GW) A unit of power (equals 1 billion watts or 1 million kilowatts or 1,000 megawatts).

Grid-connected system A solar electric system that is integrated into the utility power service system.

Grid Lines Contacts on the surface of a PV cell to provide a low resistance path for electrons to flow out.

High voltage disconnect The electrical voltage level that, when encountered, causes the charge controller to disconnect the battery from the photovoltaic system.

Hybrid system A solar electric system integrated with a wind generator or other power source.

Hydrogenated amorphous silicon Silicon containing a small amount of hydrogen to allow charge carriers to flow more freely.

Input voltage The power required by an electrical load.

Interconnect A conductor connecting two or more solar cells.

Inverter A device that changes DC electrical current to AC current, usually so it can operate AC-powered electrical equipment.

Ion An atom that has lost or gained electrons and become positively or negatively charged.

Joule A metric unit of energy; 1 joule per second equals 1 watt (or 0.737 foot-pounds); 1 Btu equals 1,055 joules.

Kilowatt (kW) A unit of electrical power equal to 1000 watts.

Kilowatt-Hour (kWh) 1,000 watts acting over a period of 1 hour. Used mostly as a measure on utility bills.

Lead-acid battery A battery with pure lead plates, lead-antimony, or lead-calcium in an acid electrolyte.

Load The equipment or component in an electrical circuit that is the consumer of the power.

Low voltage warning A buzzer or light that signals battery voltage has dropped below a set point.

Maintenance-free battery A sealed battery with an electrolyte that cannot be replenished.

Megawatt (MW) 1,000 kilowatts or 1 million watts; used to list the capacity of electric power plants.

Multicrystalline A semiconductor material composed of small, individual crystals. Also called polycrystalline or semicrystalline.

Multi-stage controller A charge controller device that adjusts charging current according to a battery's state of charge.

N-Type Semiconductor material (silicon) with a negative charge (surplus of electrons).

Ohm A unit of measure of electrical resistance in which the potential difference of 1 volt produces a current of 1 amp.

Orientation PV panel placement relative to compass directions.

Panel See photovoltaic (PV) panel.

Parallel connection To join solar cells or photovoltaic units by connecting the positive leads in one series and the negative leads in another.

Peak sun hour The time it takes for solar irradiance to amount to 1,000 watts over an area of one square meter.

Phosphorous (P) A chemical element used in making n-type semiconductors.

Photocurrent A radiant electrical current.

Photoelectric cell A device for measuring light intensity.

Photon A particle of light.

Photovoltaic (PV) Converting light to electricity.

Photovoltaic (PV) array A system of solar panels that cooperatively produce electrical current.

Photovoltaic (PV) cell A single semiconductor element within a PV grouping.

Photovoltaic (PV) effect The basis of solar power collection: photons in light beams displace electrons that are captured and harnessed to convert to voltage.

Photovoltaic (PV) panel A panel made up of multiple PV modules for the purpose of collecting photocurrent.

Polycrystalline silicon A mineral used to construct photovoltaic cells.

P-Type A positive semiconductor (silicon) with a deficit of electrons.

PV See photovoltaic.

Regulator A device that prevents the overcharging of batteries.

Resistance The effect, measured in ohms, that occurs when a conductor opposes electrical flow, resulting in the generation of heat.

Reverse current protection Prevents current in the battery from flowing back to its source.

Sealed battery A battery with an electrolyte that cannot be replenished.

Secondary battery Any rechargeable battery.

Self-discharge The natural loss of current in a stored battery.

Semiconductor A material that conducts electricity but with resistance in a very specific range.

Series connection Joining photovoltaic cells by connecting positive leads to negative leads.

Shallow-cycle battery A small-plate battery that can withstand only limited charge/discharge cycles.

Silicon (Si) A semiconducting chemical element used in the manufacture of photovoltaic devices.

Single-crystal silicon Type of silicon commonly used to make PV cells.

Solar panel See photovoltaic (PV) panel.

Stand-alone system A freestanding electrical distribution system that is not integrated with another power source or any other power grid system.

State-of-Charge (SOC) The amount of voltage available in a battery.

Substrate The base material on which PV cells are housed.

Thermophotovoltaic Cell (TPV) A device that is heated by absorbed sunlight to produce thermal radiation that assists in conversion in a PV cell.

Thin film A layer of semiconductor material that is used in the manufacture of photovoltaic cells.

Tracking array A grouping of PV panels that rotate and move to track the position of the sun for maximum solar gain.

Transformer An electromagnetic device that steps down the voltage of alternating current.

Trickle charge To apply charge at a low rate that compensates for discharge in a stored battery.

Underground Feeder (UF) Exterior-rated electrical cable that may be used as wiring in a photovoltaic array.

Vented cell A battery with a mechanism for expelling gases.

Volt (V) A unit of electrical force that will cause a current of one amp to flow through a resistance of one ohm.

Voltage protection A feature that will disconnect a battery if input voltage limits are exceeded.

Watt Energy transfer rate of one amp under an electrical pressure of one volt. The product of voltage and current (amperage).

Conversions

METRIC EQUIVALENT

Inches (in.)	1/64	1/32	1/25	1/16	1/8	1/4	3/8	2/5	1/2	5/8	3/4	7/8	1	2	3	4	5	6	7	8	9	10	11	12	36	39.4
Feet (ft.)																								1	3	3½
Yards (yd.)																									1	1½
Millimeters (mm)	0.40	0.79	1	1.59	3.18	6.35	9.53	10	12.7	15.9	19.1	22.2	25.4	50.8	76.2	101.6	127	152	178	203	229	254	279	305	914	1,000
Centimeters (cm)							0.95	1	1.27	1.59	1.91	2.22	2.54	5.08	7.62	10.16	12.7	15.2	17.8	20.3	22.9	25.4	27.9	30.5	91.4	100
Meters (m)																								.30	.91	1.00

CONVERTING MEASUREMENTS

TO CONVERT:	TO:	MULTIPLY BY:
Inches	Millimeters	25.4
Inches	Centimeters	2.54
Feet	Meters	0.305
Yards	Meters	0.914
Square inches	Square centimeters	6.45
Square feet	Square meters	0.093
Square yards	Square meters	0.836
Ounces	Milliliters	30.0
Pints (U.S.)	Liters	0.473 (Imp. 0.568)
Quarts (U.S.)	Liters	0.946 (Imp. 1.136)
Gallons (U.S.)	Liters	3.785 (Imp. 4.546)
Ounces	Grams	28.4
Pounds	Kilograms	0.454

TO CONVERT:	TO:	MULTIPLY BY:
Millimeters	Inches	0.039
Centimeters	Inches	0.394
Meters	Feet	3.28
Meters	Yards	1.09
Square centimeters	Square inches	0.155
Square meters	Square feet	10.8
Square meters	Square yards	1.2
Milliliters	Ounces	.033
Liters	Pints (U.S.)	2.114 (Imp. 1.76)
Liters	Quarts (U.S.)	1.057 (Imp. 0.88)
Liters	Gallons (U.S.)	0.264 (Imp. 0.22)
Grams	Ounces	0.035
Kilograms	Pounds	2.2

CONVERTING TEMPERATURES

Convert degrees Fahrenheit (F) to degrees Celsius (C) by following this simple formula: Subtract 32 from the Fahrenheit temperature reading. Then, multiply that number by $\frac{5}{9}$. For example, 77°F – 32 = 45. 45 × $\frac{5}{9}$ = 25°C.

To convert degrees Celsius to degrees Fahrenheit, multiply the Celsius temperature reading by $\frac{9}{5}$. Then, add 32. For example, 25°C × $\frac{9}{5}$ = 45. 45 + 32 = 77°F.

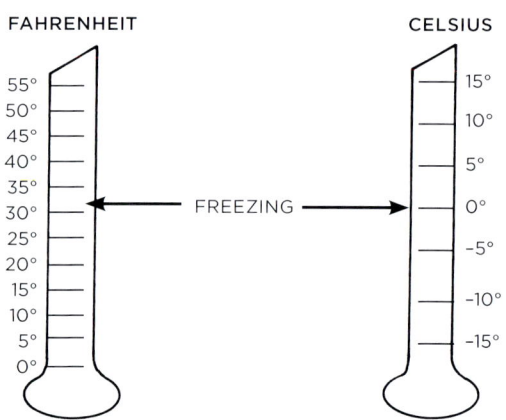

DRILL BIT GUIDE

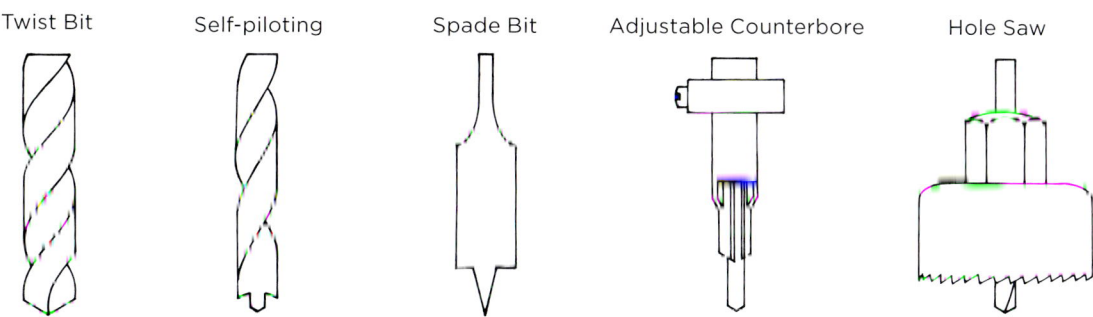

Twist Bit   Self-piloting   Spade Bit   Adjustable Counterbore   Hole Saw

NAILS

Nail lengths are identified by numbers from 4 to 60 followed by the letter "d," which stands for "penny." For general framing and repair work, use common or box nails. Common nails are best suited to framing work where strength is important. Box nails are smaller in diameter than common nails, which makes them easier to drive and less likely to split wood. Use box nails for light work and thin materials. Most common and box nails have a cement or vinyl coating that improves their holding power.

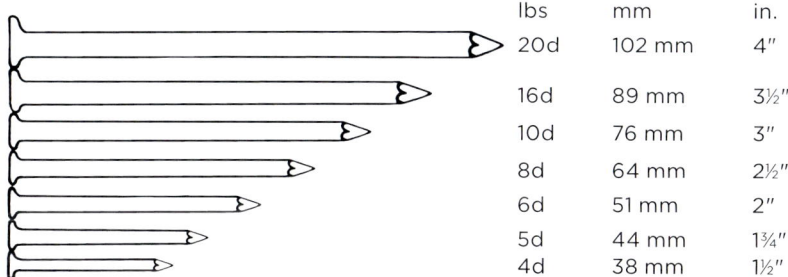

lbs	mm	in.
20d	102 mm	4"
16d	89 mm	3½"
10d	76 mm	3"
8d	64 mm	2½"
6d	51 mm	2"
5d	44 mm	1¾"
4d	38 mm	1½"

COUNTERBORE, SHANK & PILOT HOLE DIAMETERS

Screw Size	Counterbore Diameter for Screw Head	Clearance Hole for Screw Shank	Pilot Hole Diameter Hard Wood	Soft Wood
#1	⁵⁄₃₂	⁵⁄₆₄	⁵⁄₆₄	¹⁄₃₂
#2	¼	³⁄₃₂	³⁄₆₄	¹⁄₃₂
#3	¼	⁷⁄₆₄	¹⁄₁₆	³⁄₆₄
#4	¼	⅛	¹⁄₁₆	³⁄₆₄
#5	¼	⁹⁄₆₄	⁵⁄₆₄	¹⁄₁₆
#6	⁵⁄₁₆	⁵⁄₃₂	³⁄₃₂	⁵⁄₆₄
#7	⁵⁄₁₆	⁵⁄₃₂	³⁄₃₂	⁵⁄₆₄
#8	⅜	¹¹⁄₆₄	⅛	³⁄₃₂
#9	⅜	¹¹⁄₆₄	⅛	³⁄₃₂
#10	⅜	³⁄₁₆	⅛	⁷⁄₆₄
#11	½	³⁄₁₆	⁵⁄₃₂	⁹⁄₆₄
#12	½	⁷⁄₃₂	⁹⁄₆₄	⅛

Index